Rebbe Nachman's
תיקון הכללי
Tikkun
The complete remedy

Rebbe Nachman's

תיקון הכללי
Tikkun

The complete remedy

In memory of

R' Moshe Manes
ben
Yaakov Yitzchok Horn *z"l*

Devorah & Dov Elias

Some Thoughts on the Tikkun HaKlali

Based on R. Noson's Preface

What is the connection between physically losing seed and reciting ten psalms? In what way can they be a "remedy"? And why should the Ten Psalms which Rebbe Nachman specified be called the Tikkun Klali, the "complete" or "comprehensive" remedy?

At times, as Rebbe Nachman pointed out,[1] the emission of seed at night can happen purely accidentally. It may have been caused merely by eating certain foods or sleeping in a bad position. But at other times the individual himself is responsible. He encouraged himself by allowing himself to dwell on certain thoughts and fantasies. In this case, the emission is more than merely a physical occurrence. There is a spiritual dimension to it. This person has allowed a distortion to enter into his relation to his sexuality, which should in reality be treated with the utmost sanctity.

Creation

Nowhere is the greatness of God revealed more magnificently than in the creation of life. In the act of procreation, man becomes God's partner. It is a privileged role, and for this reason every detail of the act of procreation has to be invested with supreme reverence and purity. The forces involved are very powerful. Therefore God has bound us with a Covenant which obligates us to act with restraint and holiness. The mark of Covenant is a sign of the favor God has shown us in appointing us His partners.

It is a precious thing when man harnesses his physical urges within the harmony of a life founded on the guidance of Torah. Then the union of husband and wife becomes a sublime expression of their love for each other – love deepened by their mutual love of God. Their lives are a partnership with God. All the vitality of their souls is given over to the work of creation and building, fulfilling the commandments of God.

Joy

The key to this approach to life is joy. The more we deepen our faith in God the more we understand that Godliness is to be found in all things. We learn that everything we do has a special significance both for our own personal spiritual growth and in the total process through which God reveals Himself to His creation. If we understand the privileged place which we, as Jews, have within this scheme, we can be filled with joy in whatever we do. No matter what God may send us, we know that it is for the best, even if we cannot yet understand how. Joy gives us the strength to go further on our spiritual path.

But the forces connected with sexuality are double-edged. For when they are allowed to become separated from their true purpose they can push people to terrible forms of degradation. The purpose of the sexual act is the creation of life. Carrying it out purely for the sake of gratification betrays a callous disregard for the preciousness of life. People who act this way may give the outward appearance of seeking closeness to a partner. But in reality they are looking for situations in which their own desires will be gratified. Nowhere is this more evident than with masturbation, which can be carried out in solitude and has no connection with procreation at all. The seed literally goes to waste.

Depression

Yet even when gratification comes, it can never truly satisfy. Because what is really driving the individual on is a gnawing dissatisfaction with himself, a sense of depression and frustration caused by the awareness deep down that he is not fulfilling himself as God wishes. He seeks solace for his dissatisfaction in superficial pleasure, but they only make him more frustrated, driving him on further. This is why the futile search for gratification can become so compulsive, dominating all of a person's thoughts, his speech and his actions. The whole complex may be buried beneath a surface veneer of "contentment". But because he fails truly to fulfill his role in the scheme of things, he is far from the experience of genuine joy. God remains hidden from him.

The Realm of the Kelipot

   If God is hidden, it is to encourage man to search for Him – and he develops and strengthens himself in the process. God intended that man should earn his closeness to God – which is the truest good – through his own efforts. Therefore God gave man free will and set him in a world which contains evil as well as good. In this world, the option of doing good is rarely completely obvious and clear-cut. Man's mission is to distinguish the good from the bad and by an act of will to choose the good. Now since that which is good and which aspires to God was to be made less obvious, it was necessary for Godliness to be concealed.

   The sages of the Torah have expressed this idea of the concealment of Godliness through the image of a piece of fruit, in which the sweet flesh inside is covered with a hard exterior peel or shell, in Hebrew a *kelipah*.[2] Evil hovers close to the place of the good, and it has to be stripped away and discarded in order for the good to be revealed. Just as there are many different aspects to Godliness, so are there many different grades of *kelipot*. For example, when a person eats, he can devote the vitality he derives from his food to holy activities – the fulfillment of mitzvot, the study of Torah, earning a living in order to give charity, etc.[3] On the other hand he could become side-tracked from these purposes if, for example, he became overly concerned with enjoying his food, even at the expense of his health. In this case his desire for something secondary – the taste of the food – has become a *kelipah* holding him back from his true objective as a Jew. If he indulges his desire until it becomes habitual and he feels that he cannot live without satisfying it, he has given part of his very life-force up to the power of the *kelipah*.[4]

Kelipot exist over the entire range of human activities – in the form of all the temptations, obstacles, misconceptions, confusion etc. which can distract man from his mission. Strongest of all are the *kelipot* connected with the realm of sexuality, which have the power to conceal its true significance completely from men's consciousness.[5] Instead of fulfilling the role God has given in its greatness and beauty, they become distracted by the secondary, the superficial, the immediate. It is dangerously easy to get caught in the spiraling syndrome of superficial gratification, frustration and depression. The sages of the Torah, who had profound insight into human psychology, taught that the name of the *kelipah* at the core of this syndrome is לילית *Lilith*. One of the shades of meaning which this name conveys is that of a howling cry – *yelalah* – the cry of man's pain, depression and despair. A person who is at the mercy of his fantasies and desires and who follows them wherever they point can really be said to be held captive by the *kelipah*. More and more of his energy becomes invested in patterns which are ultimately destructive, and the source of his energy, his vital soul, becomes sapped.

The Remedy

At times it may be relatively easy to identify the *kelipah* for what it is and to make a determined effort of will to resist it. But at other times the *kelipah* may seem so hard and intractable that a person may, in his frailty, imagine that only the *kelipah* has any reality. It can impose itself on his consciousness so strongly – in the form of intense desires, confusion, or intractable obstacles, etc. – that he is unable to see that the *kelipah* is no more than an instrument created by God for the purpose of placing man in a situation of choice. But however compelling the power of the *kelipah* may seem, it is ultimately subordinate to the supreme power of God. The remedy, then, is to strengthen our awareness that everything that exists was created by God. In His love and strength He is always close by to release us from the pressures and troubles which surround us. Even when a person becomes overwhelmed by the temptation to choose evil, God's desire is not to punish him but to enable him to return to his senses and choose what is truly best for him.

When a person recognizes that he has given over part of his life-force to the *kelipot*, the first step is for him to acknowledge his wrong for what it was.

At the time of his wrong-doing he may have been so overcome by the intensity of his desire that he pretended what he did was permissible. He may have made the mistake of supposing that the *kelipah* had independent power of its own. By confessing now, he acknowledges that what he did was all the time forbidden by God. In this way he has "returned the kingship to God," and he has again become aware of God's ultimate power.[6]

Language

The confession and the acknowledgement in words are important, because man is first and foremost a creature of language.[7] This involves more than the mere fact that he expresses himself in words. Action is also bound up with language, because all action has a meaning, which can be expressed in language. Thoughts also, even the most subtle processes of thinking, always enter our consciousness clothed in language.[8] Because of the centrality of language in our lives, the concepts which we possess have a decisive influence over everything that we think, say or do.

Language can reveal or conceal. Even on the simplest level, we can say that a cup is half full or half empty.[9] Whatever we say about life and its situations, the words we use express an entire system of belief and outlook. We may speak in a way which brings out how the whole of life, with all its details, is a quest to reveal Godliness. Or we may try to hide the fact beneath a façade of ideology, rationalization and pseudo-explanation so complicated that it is almost impossible to identify the falsehoods on which the whole edifice has been constructed.[10] If we are to lead our lives as we should, we have to put our ideas – and therefore our language – in order: to know the truths of our existence and our condition, and to know that everything in our lives has been sent by God.[11] So even when things are dark and we seem to be encompassed by confusion, frustration, obstacles and threats, God is with us. It is He who has sent the situation and He who will draw us out of it.

The Holy Tongue

The Hebrew word for Psalms, Tehilim, has the numerical value of 485, which is equivalent to that of Lilith, the name of the evil spirit appointed over the kelipah which captured the seed. While reciting the psalms, one should keep in mind that the word Tehilim, numerically 485, corresponds to the two divine names El and Elohim. It is these two names which have the power to release the seed from the kelipah. The seed embodies the divine attributes of chessed, love, and gevurah, strength, because the seed contains the power of fire and water, heat and liquid, and these correspond to love and strength. Through the two names El and Elohim, which function using chessed and gevurah respectively and which are numerically equivalent to Tehillim, the seed is released from the kelipah.

The sages of the Torah said that the world was created through the letters of the Holy Tongue. One of the implications of this is that all the realities of our existence are actually contained within the words of the Hebrew language and the letters which make them up. It is not that the language merely mirrors a pre-existing reality. The language actually possesses creative power itself. For this reason the Holy Tongue expresses the wisdom of the Creator and the design which He has laid down as the pattern for the entire creation. This design is visible in the very perfection of the Holy Tongue itself, where the relationships between concepts can be illustrated numerically by *gematria*. Although there are various different methods of *gematria*, none of them is arbitrary. Valid conclusions can only be drawn by a scholar with a profound understanding of the Hebrew language and the mystical levels of Torah.[12]

In the lesson about the Ten Psalms, Rebbe Nachman shows that even though the *kelipah* Lilith may at times seem so powerful that it takes on the appearance of an independent force which captures the seed, in reality this power can be undermined by the power of the *kelipah*'s counterpart in the realm of holiness. This is the holiness embodied in the Psalms. The way in which the one is a counterpart of the other is brought out by showing that the numerical values of the two words are the same. Rebbe Nachman draws attention to the powerful forces involved in sexuality when he mentions that the seed embodies the divine attributes of *chessed* and *gevurah*, love and strength. Indeed it is God's love and strength which have the power to release man from the hold of the *kelipah* – a fact which is illustrated by showing how the word *Tehilim* is numerically equivalent to the two names of God which express these two aspects, *El* and *Elohim*.

Song

All of our activity is governed by language, and in order to remedy the problems in our lives we have to put our language and our ideas in order. But that is not to say that the process is purely intellectual. It is one in which man has to work on all the varied levels of his being, spiritual, intellectual, emotional, instinctive, etc. He has to draw upon all the powers of his soul in order to work upon himself and change himself. And the language of the soul is song.

We know intuitively the great power of song to come across and stir our very being. The greatness of a singer is a measure of his power to communicate with the widest range of men and women and penetrate to the most hidden depths of their souls and rouse them. It is in this sense that King David is called the "sweet singer of Israel" (Samuel II 23:1). The *Tzadik* has the power to see into the souls of all Jews[13], to see the depression and frustration caused by the exile – the physical exile to foreign lands and the spiritual exile into the hold of lust, desire and futility.

And more than this, the *Tzadik* has the power to penetrate even beneath this to the vital spark, the "good point", which is itself the victim of this exile.[14] The *Tzadik* has the skill to communicate with this spark and arouse it. The words of his song are words of truth, which look the realities of life in the face and show how they are filled with goodness and hope.

The Ten Forms of Song:

The reason why it is necessary to recite ten psalms is that there are ten forms of song corresponding to the ten expressions of song and praise on which the book of Psalms is based (see Pesachim 117a; Zohar III 101a), namely Ashrei, LamNatseach, Maskil, Halleluyah, etc. (see Rashi on Pesachim loc. cit.). Each of these expressions has the power to nullify the power of the kelipah because each of them is the direct opposite of the kelipah. Ashrei, for example, is an expression for sight and vision, the opposite of the kelipah, whose main strength lies in damaging people's vision... Ashrei, an expression of vision, is therefore the opposite of the kelipah. Similarly in the case of the expression MaSKiL, the kelipah is MeShaKel, "making childless" – the kelipah damages and spoils. MaSKiL, which means "making wise", counters this. The source of the power of the

> *kelipah to make a person sin and experience a night-time pollution derives from the language of the Targum, translation, and there is a concept of one who is "wise (Maskil) from hearing translation." In such a case good and evil are mixed up. At times he is MeShaKeL, at others MaSKiL.*
>
> *Similarly Halleluyah, an expression of praise and joy, counters the howl – yelalah – which gives the kelipah its name of Lilith, because she constantly howls. Halleli, praise, is the opposite of yelalah.*

In this section of the lesson, Rebbe Nachman explains how it is that the ten forms of song mentioned in the Talmud have the power to conquer the forces of depression. There are certain fundamental weaknesses to which men are susceptible as part of the human condition. These weaknesses are rooted in the *kelipot*. But each of the forms of song has a power which can grapple with one of these weaknesses, with the one which is, as it were, its opposite number in the realm of the *kelipot*. Through the Ten Psalms which express the ten forms of song, spiritual power rooted in the realm of holiness is channeled to counter the power of the forces of evil.

Thus the word *Ashrei*, which is usually translated as "Happy", has a connotation of vision and perception. (*Ashrei* is related to the Hebrew root Shur, which means to "travel around", "look around," and "view", etc.) Rebbe Nachman points out that the main power of the *kelipah* comes from distortions in men's vision. It is only when we fail to perceive unity that underlies the apparent diversity of this world that we allow ourselves to be deceived by this world. When we are blind to the way in which all things point to a common source and purpose, we inevitably become disconnected from that Source. Yet all true joy derives only from here. If out of depression we turn for solace to the superficial – to immediate "gratification" or easy "solutions" etc., we give over our life-force to powers which can never bring true fulfillment.

The remedy is to correct our faulty vision and achieve a shift in perception which will enable us to understand the real nature and purpose of the world we live in. The only way to achieve true happiness – to be *Ashrei* – is if we correct our vision and perception of the world.

Man is placed in a world in which good is mixed up with evil. He has to *interpret* his environment in order to choose how to respond to it. It is significant that the word *Maskil* has two very contradictory meanings depending on the way it is vocalized. The consonants which make up the Hebrew root can be read as *MaSKiL*, which means "being wise." Or they can be read as *MeShaKel*, which means "bringing about a miscarriage", "making childless." Since the Hebrew word is usually written without the vowel points, it is up to the reader to *interpret* the correct meaning from the context.

Rashi on Psalms 32:1 comments that the sages said that every Psalm beginning with the word *Maskil* was "said through an interpreter". Thus, it was a level at which people could have some grasp of it. But the process of interpretation or translation is not without its dangers. There is always the risk of *mis*-interpreting or *mis*-translating. It is possible to stray very far from the true goal and even to come to disaster.

If we become skilled in interpreting the things which happen to us in life, we can profit greatly from this world. We can understand the true significance of its tests and challenges and we know what to choose and what to reject. We will not be deceived by temptations. And even if we suffer, we will understand that our troubles are sent by God for our own good and we will not chaff. To know how to interpret the world around us is to be wise. The book of Proverbs (19, 14) speaks of – אשה משכלת – a "wise woman" a reference to the spark of Godliness within us which is the source of our divine intelligence. But this same word can also be read as – משכלת – a destructive woman who causes miscarriage and death. It can be highly dangerous to mistake the true significance of this world to embrace temptation as if it could lead to genuine satisfaction, to run from the slightest difficulty as if solace could be found in falsehood. In this case the *kelipah* which is the source of the misinterpretation is *MeShaKeLeT*: it can leave people spiritually and physically stunted and childless.

The word *Halleluyah* is the fullest expression of praise and thanksgiving to God. The culmination of the book of Psalms in the last chapter is a resounding succession of praises. "All that has breath, praise God. *Halleluyah.*" The whole of existence sings out to God. The revelation is total and complete. There is nowhere that the presence of God remains hidden and concealed. At last the forces of the *kelipot* are completely vanquished. Indeed the greatest joy of all is the joy that emerges out of darkness and despair.

The voice of the *kelipah*, which clouds over the radiance of God with a veil of darkness, is *yelalah*: a howl of pain and despair. It is a cry which at times we can hear with chilling effect from the lips of men. At other times, the cry is stifled. People find they can no longer cry. The words are stuck in the throat. But in time to come, when the triumph of Godliness is complete, the *YeLaLaH* of the *kelipah* will be turned into *HaLLelY*, praise.

Each of the other expressions of song can also be shown to have the power to counter one of the aspects of the *kelipot* which throw men into hopelessness and despair. Depression is the fundamental sickness of the soul. It is the source of the desperation which drives people to sin. Each individual sin is a wound of the soul which has its own particular remedy. But the individual sores are really symptomatic of a deeper sickness. If this can be remedied it will restore the health of the whole. The remedy lies in the joy of a soul singing the praises of God. This is the comprehensive remedy.

Each of the Ten Psalms which make up the *Tikkun HaKlali* is a powerful song and a powerful teaching. May we be worthy of saying the words with simplicity, sincerely and thoughtfully. Let them enter the fabric of our being. Let us ponder them, meditating on their meaning and opening ourselves to their healing powers. Let us be responsive to the music and joy of these songs until our pains, our fears, our anxieties and despair are banished and we will see only the goodness of the Living God through the merit of our Righteous Messiah. Amen.

---

1 Above p. 23

2 cf. Zohar I 19b

3 *Likutey Moharan* II, 16

4 Ibid. I, 62

5 Ibid. 2

6 *Likutey Moharan* I, 4

7 Thus the Hebrew words "and the man became a living soul" (Genesis 2:7) are translated by the Aramaic Targum "and the man became a *speaking* soul".

8 *Likutey Moharan* I, 4

9 cf. *Likutey Moharan* I, 51

10 *Likutey Moharan* I, 38

11 Ibid.

12 See *Rebbe Nachman's Wisdom* 203

13 *Rebbe Nachman's Wisdom* 185

14 *Likutey Moharan* I, 282; *Rebbe Nachman's Wisdom* 273

The Holy Covenant:
Comments by the Sages

"It is forbidden to masturbate, and this sin is more serious than any other sin in the Torah." (*Tur, Shulchan Aruch, Even Ha-ezer* 23:1).

"R. Eliezer said: 'It is written, "Your hands are full of blood" (Isaiah 1:15). This refers to people who arouse themselves with their hands. The words of the commandment, "You shall not commit adultery" (Ex. 20:13) imply: not with your hand, and not with your foot." (*Niddah* 13b).

"This is the way of the Evil Inclination. Today he tells you, "Do this," and tomorrow, "go and serve idols" (*Niddah* 13b). The *Iyun Yaakov* explains that this is all for the sake of immorality, to provide a rationalization for open sexual license.

" 'You shall not go astray after your hearts and after your eyes': (Nu. 15:39). 'After your hearts' – this refers to atheism. 'After your eyes' – this refers to sexual immorality." (*Berachot* 12b).

"The eye and the heart are the two middlemen of sin: the eye sees, the heart desires, and the body completes the action." (Rashi on Numbers 25:39).

"R. Yochanan said, 'Anyone who wastes his seed is liable to the death penalty, as it is written, "And the thing which he did was evil in the sight of Hashem, and He slew him also." (Genesis 38:10)" (*Niddah* 13a).

"R. Yitzchak and R. Ami said, 'It is as if he were a murderer, as it is written, "Slaughterers of children in the valleys, under the clefts of the rocks." (Is. 57:5)'" (*Niddah ibid.*)

"R. Asi said, 'It is as if he were an idol-worshipper." (*Ibid.*)

"A person should not entertain lustful thoughts by day, lest he come to impurity at night." (*Avodah Zarah* 20b).

"Sinful thoughts are worse than the sin itself." (*Yoma* 20a).

"Rabbi Simlai said, 'Wherever there is immorality, indiscriminate destruction comes into the world and kills the good with the wicked." (*Bereshit Rabba* 26).

"The Holy One, blessed-be-He, is slow to anger with regard to everything except immorality." (Ibid.)

"Great is circumcision, over which thirteen covenants were struck." (*Nedarim* 31b).

"But for circumcision, the Holy One, blessed-be-He, would not have created the world, as it is written,

'If My covenant be not observed day and night, it were as if I had not appointed the ordinance of heaven and earth'. " (*Ibid.*)

When a person comes to make himself impure, the doors are opened for him; when he comes to purify himself, he is assisted. Sin sullies the heart of man and makes it insensitive. When a man makes himself a little impure, (his penalty is that) he is made very impure. If he makes himself impure in the world below, he is made impure in the worlds above. If he makes himself impure in this world, he is made impure in the World to Come. But if he sanctifies himself a little, [his reward is that] he is given great sanctity. If he sanctifies himself in this world, he is sanctified in the World to Come (*Yoma* 38b).

The angel presiding over Gehinnom is called Duma. Under him are tens of thousands of destroying angels. He stands at the entrance to Gehinnom. But to those who guarded the Holy Covenant in this world, he has no power to approach. (Zohar I 8a).

Whoever observes this Covenant on which the world is established is called "righteous." We learn this from Joseph, who because he observed the Covenant is known as Joseph the Righteous. (*Ibid.* 59b).

As long as Israel observe the Holy covenant they cause stability in the world, above and below. But when they forsake the Covenant there is no stability above or below. (*Ibid.* 66b).

As long as men remain attached to this Covenant and do not forsake it, there is no race or tongue that can harm them. (*Ibid.*)

There is no sin in the world which angers the Holy One, blessed-be-He, as much as that of neglecting the Covenant, as it is written, "A sword that will execute the vengeance of the Covenant." (Lev. 26:25) (*Ibid.*)

When a person guards the holy Covenant, it is as if he had observed the entire Torah, because the Covenant is equal to the whole Torah. (*Ibid.* I 197a).

The Holy covenant makes the body of man radiant and lustrous, and one who guards it will never come to any harm. (*Ibid.* II 3b).

When a person denies the Holy Covenant which is sealed in his flesh, it is as if he denied the name of the Holy One, blessed-be-He, and one who denies the seal of the King is as if he denies the King himself. (*Ibid.*)

When a person guards the Covenant, it is as if he had observed the entire Torah, but if he denies it, it is as if he denies the entire Torah. (*Ibid.* III 13b).

Gentiles, before they are circumcised, abide in the lower crowns which are not holy, and an impure spirit rests upon them; but when they are converted and circumcised, they dwell in the crowns of holiness. (*Ibid.* III 14b).

The Torah is called a "Covenant", the Holy One, blessed-be-He is called "Covenant," and this holy sign is called "Covenant". (*Ibid.* III 73b).

Whoever guards the Holy Covenant is worthy of kingship – like Joseph. Thus Israel, because they observe the Covenant, are worthy of kingship, and it is said of them that 'All Israel are the sons of kings.' (*Tikkuney Zohar* 51a, Tikkun 15).

Whoever guards the sign of the Covenant in every place that it is present – in the sign of the circumcision, in the Sabbath and festivals – is protected by the Holy One blessed-be-He in whatever place he is, and he is guarded against his enemies (*Tikkuney Zohar* 87a Tikkun 21).

When a person guards the Covenant, which is His seal, death departs from him. (*Tikkuney Zohar* 96, Tikkun 22)

When a person guards the Covenant, the Holy One blessed-be-He gives him a child about whom it is written "And Hashem God caused every tree of lovely appearance to sprout forth" (Gen. 2:9) – this refers to the secrets of Torah. (*Tikkuney Zohar* 124a, Tikkun 47)

The Gravity of the sin of the willful emission of seed:

"And the earth was corrupt," (Gen. 6:11). If men sinned, why should the earth be called corrupt? The explanation is that it is mankind that is the essence of the earth, so they cause the earth to become corrupt if they themselves are corrupt. This is made clear by the words of the Torah: "And God saw the earth, and behold it was corrupt, because all flesh had corrupted their way upon the earth." (*Ibid.* 12). For indeed all the other sins of man, which involve only his own corruption, can be atoned for with repentance. But the sin of willfully emitting seed is one by which man corrupts both himself and the earth. Of such a person it is written, "The stain of your iniquity remains before me" (Jer. 2:22), "For You are not a God that has pleasure in wickedness: evil will not sojourn with You" (Ps. 5:5).

(*Zohar* I 62a)

A person should be on guard against sin and he should be careful about his actions before the Holy One, blessed-be-He. There are many messengers in this world that travel and move about, and bear witness to men's actions. All of them are recorded in a book. The sin which defiles man more than any other, both in this world and in the World to Come is the sin of wasting seed. A man who is guilty of this will not enter within the Heavenly Curtain and will not enter the presence of the Ancient of Days. "For you are not a God that has pleasure in wickedness: evil will not sojourn with You" (Ps. 5;5). (*Ibid* 188a).

Rabbi Yitzchak said, "One who willfully spills his seed, like Er the son of Judah, is thrust down lower than all the others in Gehinnom. All others have a chance to ascend except him. Is he worse than a murderer? A murderer kills another man's children, but he kills his own, and he spills very much blood." Rabbi Judah said: "Every sin can be atoned for through repentance except for this, and every sinner may hope to see the face of the Shechinah except for this one." (*Ibid.* 219b).

The Zohar states that repentance does not help for the sin of spilling one's seed in vain. The Rebbe said that this is not so. Repentance helps for all sins. He also said that no one understands the meaning of this passage in the Zohar except for him. The truth is that repentance certainly helps for this sin, even if one has carried out this sin many times. True repentance involves never repeating the sin again. You must go to the same place and be exposed to the same temptation. Only this time you must take care not to do the same thing as you did before. You must break your desire and withstand the temptation. This is the essence of repentance. (*Rebbe Nachman's Wisdom* 71).

The holy drop which emerges from the foundation, which is the place of the Covenant, is the light of the holy "point". It is forbidden to expel it unless in the context of holy union, because otherwise it is tantamount to destroying the world. The reason why it is stated that *teshuva* – repentance – is impossible for one who spills his seed is because he has nowhere to return *to*. Where should he return now that he has ruined the "point" itself, which is the very root of his vitality? *Teshuva* is possible as long as a person's "point" remains intact. But as for one who ruins his point and, as it were, uproots it God forbid: where should he return? And yet, the truth of the matter is that "nothing stands in the way of *teshuva*," as is mentioned throughout the holy literature. If a person repents he will surely be forgiven. But in essence his *teshuva* can come about only with the help of the Tzadik of the era, who is the comprehensive "point" from which all the other "points" draw. This sinner who spilled his seed and ruined his own "point" is obliged to receive the light of the "point" afresh. This is only possible with the help of the Tzadik of the era, who is the root of all the "points" and who therefore has the power to radiate the "point" to him anew. For here is the root of all the "points". Strict justice demands that such a sinner should not be granted the possibility of repentance. But if he is filled with regret and pleads before God, even the repentance of one who is unworthy of being granted forgiveness will be accepted – through God's free and unstinting lovingkindness. This indeed is the remedy itself – that the sinner succeeds in arousing God's mercy so that God accepts his repentance. This penitence thereby arouses and reveals a totally new dimension of God's lovingkindness which has never before existed. The lovingkindness which exists already does not extend to granting atonement for his sin, because *teshuva*, does not help in this case. The reason is that where *teshuva* does help for sins, it is only because of God's attribute of lovingkindness, and if *teshuva* does not help for this sin, as the Zohar states, it is because the lovingkindness which exists in the world and has been revealed so far does not avail for this sin. And this is appropriate, because this sinner who has damaged the "point", which is the light of lovingkindness, has thereby damaged the light of lovingkindness itself. This is why there is no repentance for him. Therefore when God wishes to take pity upon him, He shows him a *new* lovingkindness which has never existed before. God renews his lovingkindness and reveals a new face in order to heal and forgive even one who has committed this sin. This in itself is the remedy, because a new facet of God's lovingkindness has been revealed and the sinner receives a *new* "point" through this new lovingkindness. Because the "point" *is* lovingkindness, as explained above. Through the very revelation of this new lovingkindness the sinner receives the light of the "point", which is lovingkindness, and this is his remedy. Understand this well.

The only way this remedy can come about in its entirety is through Mashiach. Mashiach will come with the remedy more especially for this sin, as it is written: "He will gather the dispersed of Judah" (Is. 12). He will gather in all the outcasts and those who have been dispersed to the four corners of the earth, and this is the remedy for this sin. For Mashiach is the light of this new lovingkindness which comes to remedy everything, as it is written, "And He does lovingkindness to his anointed one" (Ps. 18). It is written (Is. 59:20) "And a redeemer will come to Zion and to those of Jacob who return from sin." "Those who return from sin" specifically – these are the ones who repent for this sin of vain emission of seed, which is referred to (Is. 57) "Are you not children of transgression, a seed of falsehood?" It is precisely to these people that the righteous redeemer will come, because all the remedies come about precisely through him. When he comes and heals them, then the "point" will return and radiate within them. This is the meaning of the words that follow (Is. 59:21). "And as for Me. This is My covenant with them…. My spirit that is upon you and My words which I have put in your mouth…" – this refers to the "point" which dwells where the covenant of peace is observed, and this is the source of the holy spirit.

(*Likutey Halachot, Tefillin* 2, 11-12)

▪ ▪ ▪

זֶה שְׁמוֹ נָאֶה לוֹ

סֵפֶר

תִּקוּן הַכְּלָלִי

שֶׁגִּילָה הָרַב הַקָּדוֹשׁ
רַבִּי נַחְמָן מִבְּרֶסְלֶב זִיעָ"א

For further information:

Breslov Research Institute
POB 5370
Jerusalem, Israel

or:

Breslov Research Institute
POB 11
Lakewood, NJ 08701 USA

e-mail: info@breslov.org
www.breslov.org

Printed in Israel

This Sefer is dedicated in honor of the
Simchas Bar Mitzvah
of our dear son

Moishy

It is our hope and prayer that he
implements Rabbi Nachman's holy
teachings as a guide to become a true
Talmid Chacham & Yorai Shamayim

Moishy we are so proud of you
and all that you have become

Mazal Tov
Eli and Estee Kopel

* * *

I would like this dedication to be
a Zechus for the Neshamos of

my little Bubby
Chana Leah bas Shlomo Aryeh

and Gramama
Chaya Pessel bas Yissachar Dov

Moishy

Publisher's Note

Rebbe Nachman of Breslov taught that the recital of the Ten Psalms that make up his *Tikkun HaKlali* ("Complete Remedy") has many general benefits as they have the power to remedy all kinds of negative thoughts and feelings. The Ten Psalms correspond to the ten archetypal "kinds of song" which vitalize the ten basic "pulses" governing the energy system of the human soul and body as taught in the Kabbalah. Though it was originally revealed as a remedy for the damage caused by wasteful emission of seed by males, the recital of the *Tikkun HaKlali* is applicable to men and women alike.

Table of Contents

Rebbe Nachman of Breslov
(1772-1810)

Two centuries later, the teachings of Rebbe Nachman of Breslov are still very much alive. Great-grandson of the Baal Shem Tov, Rebbe Nachman is known to some as the master Chassidic story-teller. For others he is the great Kabbalist and sage who fathomed the depths of Torah with unparalleled brilliance and grace. To his followers, he is simply the "Rebbe," whose wisdom and guidance are a living force in the world today.

Rebbe Nachman was born in the Ukraine in Russia in 1772, just as the Chassidic movement was beginning to become static. He made it his mission to set Chassidism on new foundations. With the societies of his day in the ferment of change, Rebbe Nachman saw deeply into the problems of the dawning age. He wanted to reach out to all Jews, but especially to those who were remote from their tradition, to those who were perplexed or who could not understand the heritage. He spoke to those trapped in depression and despair… and to ordinary people facing the problems of everyday living. His message was one of hope and joy. He taught that even where the darkness and corruption seem most impenetrable, the sparks of life are waiting to be released.

Shortly before his passing, Rebbe Nachman told his followers that his influence will endure long after his death. *"My light will burn until the days of Mashiach."* On his passing, in 1810, he was buried in the city of Uman, mid-way between Kiev and Odessa.

His followers began to form communities devoted to following his guidance and spreading his teachings. In this century, the center of the Breslov movement shifted from the U.S.S.R. to Israel and America.

The Breslov Research Institute is devoted to keeping alive Rebbe Nachman's teachings and making them available to wider audiences. The Institute has arranged the publication of Rebbe Nachman's works and those of his followers in the original Hebrew and Yiddish, and in translations in English, French and Russian and Spanish.

הַקְדָּמָה

אִיתָא בְּלִקּוּטֵי מוֹהֲרַ"ן חֵלֶק רִאשׁוֹן סִימָן רה, וְזֶה לְשׁוֹנוֹ:
תִּקּוּן לְמִקְרֶה לַיְלָה רַחֲמָנָא לִצְּלָן, לוֹמַר עֲשָׂרָה קַפִּיטְל
תְּהִלִּים בְּאוֹתוֹ הַיּוֹם שֶׁאֵרַע לוֹ חַס וְשָׁלוֹם; כִּי יֵשׁ כֹּחַ בַּאֲמִירַת
תְּהִלִּים לְהוֹצִיא הַטִּפָּה מֵהַקְּלִפָּה שֶׁלָּקְחָה אוֹתָהּ, כִּי 'תְּהִלִּים'
בְּגִימַטְרִיָּא 'לִילִית' עִם הֶחָמֵשׁ אוֹתִיּוֹת שֶׁל שְׁמָהּ, שֶׁהִיא
הַמְמֻנָּה עַל זֶה כַּיָּדוּעַ. וְצָרִיךְ לְכַוֵּן בִּשְׁעַת אֲמִירַת תְּהִלִּים,
שֶׁ'תְּהִלִּים' בְּגִימַטְרִיָּא 'תפ"ה' שֶׁהוּא מְכֻוָּן כְּמִסְפַּר הַשְּׁנֵי
שֵׁמוֹת **אֵל אֱלֹהִים** בְּמִלּוּאוֹ, כָּזֶה: אל"ף למ"ד, אל"ף למ"ד
ה"י יו"ד מ"ם, שֶׁעַל־יְדֵי הַשְּׁנֵי שֵׁמוֹת אֵלּוּ יוֹצְאָה הַטִּפָּה
מֵהַקְּלִפָּה. כִּי הַטִּפָּה הִיא בְּחִינַת חֶסֶד וּגְבוּרָה כַּיָּדוּעַ, כִּי יֵשׁ
בָּהּ כֹּחַ אֵשׁ וּמַיִם חֲמִימוּת וְלַחוּת, שֶׁהֵם בְּחִינַת חֶסֶד וּגְבוּרָה.
וְעַל־יְדֵי הַשְּׁנֵי שֵׁמוֹת **אֵל אֱלֹהִים** הַנַּ"ל, שֶׁהֵם בְּחִינַת חֶסֶד

---

adding up the values of all the resulting letters. Thus the first of the
names, *El*, is made up of Aleph (Aleph·1 Lamed·30 Phe·80=111)
and Lamed (Lamed·30 mem·40 Dalet·4 = 74 totaling 185. *Elohim*
is Aleph (111), Lamed(74), Hey (Hey·5 Yud·10 = 15) Yud (Yud·10
Vav·6 Dalet·4 = 20) and Mem (Mem·40 Mem·40 = 80) totaling 300.
Altogether the two names give 485.

Introduction

Rebbe Nachman taught:

When a person experiences a nocturnal pollution, the *tikkun* – the remedy – is for him to recite ten psalms on the same day that it happened. Reciting psalms has the power to release the seed from the *kelipah*,[1] the evil force, which captured it. The Hebrew word for Psalms, *Tehilim*, has the numerical value of 485. This is exactly the same as the numerical value of *Lilith*, which is the name of the evil spirit appointed over the *kelipah*.[2] While reciting the psalms, one should keep in mind that the word Tehilim corresponds numerically to the two divine names *El* and *Elohim*.[3] It is these two names which have the power to release the seed from the *kelipah*. For the seed embodies the divine attributes of *chessed*, Kindness, and *gevurah*, Strength, because the seed contains the power of fire and water, heat and liquid, which correspond to Love and Strength. The two names *El* and *Elohim* are used when referring to *chessed*

---

1 See below p. *vi*.

2 The gematria of *Tehilim* is Tav·400, Hey·5 Lamed·30 Yud·10 Mem·40 = 485. *Lilith* is Lamed·30 Yud·10 Lamed·30 Yud·10 Tav·400 one unit for each letter of the name, ·5 = 485.

3 The calculation is worked out by the method of writing out each letter of the two names as that letter is itself spelled and then

וּגְבוּרָה כַּיָּדוּעַ, שֶׁהֵם גִּימַטְרִיָּא 'תְּהִלִּים' כַּנַּ"ל, עַל־יְדֵי־זֶה מוֹצִיאִין הַטִּפָּה מִשָּׁם; וְזֶה צָרִיךְ לְכַוֵּן בִּשְׁעַת אֲמִירַת תְּהִלִּים.

וְעַל כֵּן צָרִיךְ לוֹמַר עֲשָׂרָה קַפִּיטְל, כִּי יֵשׁ עֲשָׂרָה מִינֵי זִמְרָה, שֶׁהֵם בְּחִינַת הָעֲשָׂרָה לְשׁוֹנוֹת שֶׁנֶּאֱמַר בָּהֶם סֵפֶר תְּהִלִּים כַּמּוּבָא (פְּסָחִים קיז.) וּבַזֹּהַר אָמוֹר דַּף קא.), שֶׁהֵם: אַשְׁרֵי, וְלַמְנַצֵּחַ, וּמַשְׂכִּיל, וְהַלְלוּיָהּ וְכוּ', עַיֵּן בְּפֵרוּשׁ רַשִׁ"י. וְיֵשׁ כֹּחַ בְּכָל לָשׁוֹן וְלָשׁוֹן שֶׁל הָעֲשָׂרָה לְשׁוֹנוֹת הַנַּ"ל לְבַטֵּל כֹּחַ הַקְּלִפָּה הַנַּ"ל, כִּי כָּל אֶחָד מֵאֵלּוּ הַלְשׁוֹנוֹת הֵם הֵפֶךְ הַקְּלִפָּה הַנַּ"ל. כִּי 'אַשְׁרֵי' הוּא לְשׁוֹן רְאִיָּה וְהִסְתַּכְּלוּת, הֵפֶךְ הַקְּלִפָּה הַנַּ"ל, שֶׁעִקָּר כֹּחָהּ מְקַלְקֵל הָאוֹרוֹת (נֻסְחָא אַחֵר: הָרְאוּת), מִבְּחִינַת וַתִּכְהֶיןָ עֵינָיו מֵרְאֹת, בְּחִינַת 'יְהִי מְאֹרֹת' – חָסֵר, וְדָרְשׁוּ רַבּוֹתֵינוּ זַ"ל (זֹהַר בְּרֵאשִׁית דַּף לג. וְעוֹד): 'דָּא לִילִית'. נִמְצָא שֶׁעִקָּר כֹּחָהּ מְקַלְקֵל הָרְאִיָּה, וְ'אַשְׁרֵי' שֶׁהוּא לְשׁוֹן רְאִיָּה, הִיא הֵפֶךְ מִמֶּנָּה.

וְכֵן מַשְׂכִּיל, כִּי הִיא בִּבְחִינַת 'מֻשְׂכָּל', וּ'מַשְׂכִּיל' הוּא הֵפֶךְ מִזֶּה. וְעִנְיָן זֶה עַיֵּן בְּמָקוֹם אַחֵר (בְּלִקּוּטֵי א סִימָן יט), כִּי עִקָּר כֹּחָהּ לְהַחֲטִיא אֶת הָאָדָם בְּמִקְרֶה, חַס וְשָׁלוֹם, הוּא

and *gevurah* respectively. Thus it is that they have the power to release the seed from the *kelipah*. One should bear this in mind while reciting the psalms.

The reason why it is necessary to recite ten psalms is that there are ten forms of song corresponding to the ten expressions of song praise on which the book of Psalms is based (see *Pesachim* 117 and *Tikunay Zohar* 13) namely *Ashrei, Lamnatseach, Maskil, Halleluyah* etc. (see Rashi on *Pesachim* 117a). Each of these expressions has the power to nullify the strength of the *kelipah* because each of these expressions is the direct opposite of the *kelipah*. Thus the main strength of the *kelipah* lies in damaging people's vision, as we learn from the biblical verses "and his eyes were dim so that he could not see" (Gen. 27 1:14) and "let there be lights" (Gen. 1:16) is spelled without one letter when written in the Torah scroll, and can bear the interpretation of "curse". The Rabbis commented that this is an allusion to *Lilith* (*Tikuney Zohar* 44). Since the main strength of the *kelipah* lies in damaging people's vision, *Ashrei* – the first of the expressions of praise – which has the connotation of vision, is the direct opposite of the *kelipah*.

To turn to the expression *MaSkiL*, the *kelipah* is *MeShaKeL* – making childless. The *kelipah* damages and spoils. Now *MaSkiL*, which means making wise, counters this. The source of the power of the *kelipah* to make a person sin and experience a nocturnal pollution derives

עַל־יְדֵי לְשׁוֹן תַּרְגּוּם שֶׁהוּא בְּחִינַת מַשְׂכִּיל עַל־יְדֵי תֻּרְגְּמָן, שֶׁהוּא מְעֹרָב טוֹב וָרָע – לִפְעָמִים 'מְשַׂכֵּל' וְלִפְעָמִים 'מַשְׂכִּיל' עַיֵּן שָׁם.

וְכֵן 'הַלְלוּיָהּ' הֵפֶךְ הַקְּלִפָּה שֶׁשְּׁמָהּ לִילִית עַל שֵׁם שֶׁהִיא מְיַלֶּלֶת בַּלַּיְלָה תָּמִיד, וְהַלֵּל הֵפֶךְ יָלָה, כִּי אוֹתִיּוֹת 'הַלֵּלִי' הֵם הֵפֶךְ 'יָלָלָה' (וְהַשְּׁאָר לֹא פֵּרֵשׁ):

גַּם הַטִּפָּה בָּאָה מֵהַדַּעַת שֶׁהוּא בְּחִינַת חֶסֶד וּגְבוּרָה כַּיָּדוּעַ, כִּי גַם הַטִּפָּה הִיא בְּחִינַת חֶסֶד וּגְבוּרָה כַּנַּ"ל. וְיָדוּעַ שֶׁהַדַּעַת הוּא בְּחִינַת חֲמִשָּׁה חֲסָדִים וְחָמֵשׁ גְּבוּרוֹת, עַל כֵּן צָרִיךְ לוֹמַר עֲשָׂרָה קַפִּיטְל. וְזֶה בְּחִינַת (תהלים לב, א): 'לְדָוִד מַשְׂכִּיל אַשְׁרֵי נְשׂוּי פֶּשַׁע' – רָאשֵׁי תֵבוֹת 'נאף', שֶׁהוּא נִכְנַע עַל־יְדֵי בְּחִינַת 'לְדָוִד מַשְׂכִּיל', דְּהַיְנוּ תְהִלִּים, עַד כָּאן לְשׁוֹנוֹ:

from "the language of the *Targum*"[4] and a concept found in the Talmud is that of "one who is wise – *MaSKiL* – from hearing translations." In such a case, good and evil are mixed up. At times *MeShaKel*, at others *MaSKiL*.

Similarly, *HaLLeLuYah*, which is an expression of praise and joy, counters the howl, *YaLaLLaH*, which gives the *kelipah* its name of *Lilith* because of her constant howling. (Rebbe Nachman did not explain the remaining seven expressions of song and praise on which the book of Psalms is based).

The seed is derived from *da'at*, knowledge, which is the source of *chessed* and *gevurah*. (It was explained above that the seed embodies chessed and gevurah.) Now *da'at* consists of five *chassadim* and five *gevurot*, as is explained in the Kabbalah. This is the reason why it is necessary to say ten psalms. The thirty-second Psalm begins with the words *"LeDavid Maskil: Ashrei Nesui Pesha. A wise song of David. Happy is the man whose sin is forgiven."* The initial letters of the first three Hebrew words after the superscription, *Ashrei Nesui Pesha*, spell out the root-word *Na'Aph*, which denotes immorality. The force of immorality is crushed by means of *LeDavid Maskil"*, namely the Psalms.

(*Likutey Moharan* I:205)

---

4 The Targum is the translation of the Torah into Aramaic. According to the mystical works, the concept of Targum is bound up with the esoteric concept of the Tree of Knowledge (of Good and Evil). See *Likutey Moharan* I:19 for a fuller discussion.

וּבְלִקּוּטֵי תִּנְיָנָא (סִימָן צב) אִיתָא בְּזֶה הַלָּשׁוֹן: תִּקּוּן לְמִקְרֶה לַיְלָה חַס וְשָׁלוֹם, לוֹמַר עֲשָׂרָה קַפִּיטְל תְּהִלִּים כַּמְבֹאָר בַּסֵּפֶר הָרִאשׁוֹן (בְּסִימָן רה) עַיֵּן שָׁם וְכוּ'.

וְדַע כִּי זֶה הָעִנְיָן שֶׁל הָעֲשָׂרָה מִינֵי נְגִינָה הַנַּ"ל שֶׁהֵם כְּנֶגֶד פְּגַם הַנַּ"ל, הוּא מְרֻמָּז בִּפְסוּקִים אֵלּוּ: בְּרָכָה – 'אֲבָרֵךְ אֶת ה' אֲשֶׁר יְעָצָנִי אַף לֵילוֹת וְכוּ' (תהלים טז, ז); אַשְׁרֵי – 'אַשְׁרֵי נְשׂוּי פֶּשַׁע כְּסוּי חֲטָאָה' (שם לב, א); מַשְׂכִּיל – 'וּמֵה' אִשָּׁה מַשְׂכָּלֶת' (משלי יט, יד); שִׁיר – 'בַּלַּיְלָה שִׁירֹה עִמִּי'; נִצּוּחַ – 'לַמְנַצֵּחַ אַל תַּשְׁחֵת' (תהלים נט, א); נִגּוּן – 'אֶזְכְּרָה נְגִינָתִי בַּלָּיְלָה' (תהלים עז, ז); תְּפִלָּה – 'הֲיֵאָכֵל תָּפֵל מִבְּלִי מֶלַח' (איוב ו, ו); הוֹדוּ – 'פֶּן תִּתֵּן לַאֲחֵרִים הוֹדֶךָ' (משלי ה, ט); מִזְמוֹר – 'הַנֹּתֵן זְמִרוֹת בַּלָּיְלָה' (איוב לה, י); הַלְלוּיָהּ – 'אִשָּׁה יִרְאַת ה' הִיא תִתְהַלָּל' (משלי לא, ל) (וְהָבֵן הֵיטֵב רְמָזִים אֵלּוּ):

The remedy for a nocturnal pollution, God forbid, is to recite ten psalms (as explained above). The reason is that any ten psalms correspond to the ten kinds of song through which the Book of Psalms was composed (See *Pesachim* 117a; *Zohar* III, 101, 223; *Tikkuney Zohar* 13, 22), namely *Bracha, Ashrei, Maskil* etc. Now these ten kinds of song have the power to nullify the strength of the *kelipah* and the blemish caused by the impure experience. This is because they are opposite of the *kelipah* and the blemish – as explained above.

Know, that these ten types of song are alluded to in the following verses:

Bracha: "I will *bless* Hashem who has given me advice; even in the nights etc." (Psalms 16:7); *Ashrei*: "*Happy* is he whose sin is taken away, whose transgression is covered over" (Psalms 32:1); *Maskil*: "And from Hashem is a *wise* woman" (Proverbs 19:14); *Shir*: "And in the night His *song* is with me" (Psalms 42:9); *Nitzuach*: "for the *leader*: do not destroy" (Psalms 59:1); *Nigun*: "I will remember my *melody* in the night" (Psalms 77:7); *Tefilah*: "will that which has *no savor* be eaten without salt?" (Job 6:6); *Hodu*: "lest you give your *splendor* to others" (Proverbs 5:9); *Mizmor*: "The one who gives *songs* in the night" (Job 35:10); *Halilu-Yah*: "A woman who fears Hashem, she shall be *praised*" (Proverbs 31:30).

וְדַע, כִּי אֵלּוּ הֵם הָעֲשָׂרָה קַפִּיטְל תְּהִלִּים שֶׁצְּרִיכִים לְאָמְרָם
בְּאוֹתוֹ הַיּוֹם שֶׁאֵרַע לוֹ מִקְרֶה בִּלְתִּי טָהוֹר חַס וְשָׁלוֹם: מִכְתָּם
לְדָוִד – טז, לְדָוִד מַשְׂכִּיל – לֵב, אַשְׁרֵי מַשְׂכִּיל אֶל דָּל – מא,
כְּאַיָּל תַּעֲרֹג – מב, לַמְנַצֵּחַ אַל תַּשְׁחֵת – נט, לַמְנַצֵּחַ עַל
יְדוּתוּן – עז, תְּפִלָּה לְמֹשֶׁה – צ, הוֹדוּ לַה' קִרְאוּ בִשְׁמוֹ – קה,
עַל נַהֲרוֹת בָּבֶל – קלז, הַלְלוּ אֵל בְּקָדְשׁוֹ – קנ.

וְאֵלּוּ הָעֲשָׂרָה קַפִּיטְל תְּהִלִּים הֵם תִּקּוּן גָּדוֹל מְאֹד מְאֹד לָעִנְיָן
הַנַּ"ל, וּמִי שֶׁזּוֹכֶה לְאָמְרָם בְּאוֹתוֹ הַיּוֹם, אֵין צָרִיךְ לִפְחֹד עוֹד
כְּלָל מִפְּגַם הַנּוֹרָא שֶׁל הַמִּקְרֶה, חַס וְשָׁלוֹם, כִּי בְּוַדַּאי נִתְתַּקֵּן
עַל־יְדֵי־זֶה, עַד כָּאן לְשׁוֹנוֹ בְּקִצּוּר:

וְאִיתָא בְּשִׂיחוֹת הָרַ"ן (סִימָן קמא) בְּזֶה הַלָּשׁוֹן: דַע אָחִי, כִּי
בַּתְּחִלָּה אָמַר הוּא זִכְרוֹנוֹ לִבְרָכָה, הַתּוֹרָה הַנַּ"ל הַמַּתְחֶלֶת:
"תִּקּוּן לְמִקְרֶה לַיְלָה", כַּנִּדְפַּס בַּסֵּפֶר הָרִאשׁוֹן בְּסִימָן ר"ה.
וּבַתְּחִלָּה בָּעֵת שֶׁהִתְחִיל לְגַלּוֹתָהּ, לֹא הָיִיתִי לְפָנָיו אָז, אַךְ ה'
יִתְבָּרַךְ זִכַּנִי וּבָאתִי אֶצְלוֹ סָמוּךְ מְאֹד לְאוֹתָהּ הָעֵת שֶׁהִתְחִיל
לְגַלּוֹתָהּ, וְסִפֵּר לִי אֶחָד בִּשְׁמוֹ הַתּוֹרָה הַנַּ"ל כְּפִי מַה שֶּׁשָּׁמְעָה
מִפִּיו הַקָּדוֹשׁ; וּבְתוֹךְ כָּךְ, בְּאוֹתָהּ הַשָּׁעָה שֶׁשָּׁמַעְתִּי מִפִּי אַחֵר
בִּשְׁמוֹ הַתּוֹרָה הַנַּ"ל, בְּתוֹךְ כָּךְ סִבֵּב ה' יִתְבָּרַךְ שֶׁדִּבַּרְתִּי עִמּוֹ
מִזֶּה, וְחָזַר וַאֲמָרָהּ לְפָנַי בְּקִצּוּר כַּנִּדְפַּס כְּבָר בְּסִימָן ר"ה הַנַּ"ל.

Know, that the ten psalms which a person must recite on the very same day as he has an impure experience, God forbid, are:

16; 32; 41; 42; 59; 77; 90; 105; 137; 150.

These ten psalms are a very great remedy for this problem. One who is worthy of saying them on the same day need have no more fear whatsoever of the terrible blemish caused by an impure emission, because it has indubitably been corrected by this remedy without any doubt. In the merit of the remedy for this sin, our righteous Mashiach will come to gather in our scattered ones. As it is written: God builds Jerusalem, and gathers in the outcasts of Israel (Psalms 147:2). May he come speedily in our days, Amen.

(Likutey Moharan II, 92)*

▪

Rabbi Noson of Breslov (1780-1845) was Rebbe Nachman's closest student. He writes: When the Rebbe first revealed this teaching I was not present. But God caused me to come shortly afterwards and someone else told me what the Rebbe had said. Soon after this I had the opportunity to discuss it with the Rebbe personally and he repeated the ideas in brief.

וּבְאוֹתָהּ הָעֵת שֶׁנִּגְלָה הַתּוֹרָה הַנַּ"ל, לֹא גִּלָּה אָז אֵיזֶה קַפִּיטְל
לוֹמַר, רַק אָמַר סְתָם לוֹמַר עֲשָׂרָה קַפִּיטְל תְּהִלִּים לְתִקּוּן
הַנַּ"ל. וְשָׁמַעְתִּי מִפִּיו הַקָּדוֹשׁ אָז שֶׁאָמַר, שֶׁהָיָה רָאוּי לְגַלּוֹת
אֵיזֶה הֵם עֲשָׂרָה קַפִּיטְל תְּהִלִּים שֶׁצְּרִיכִין לוֹמַר; אַךְ אֵיזֶה
שֶׁהֵם עֲשָׂרָה קַפִּיטְל תְּהִלִּים שֶׁיֹּאמְרוּ, הֵם תִּקּוּן לָזֶה, כִּי כָּל
עֲשָׂרָה קַפִּיטְל תְּהִלִּים אֵיזֶה שֶׁהֵם, כֻּלָּם הֵם כְּנֶגֶד עֲשָׂרָה מִינֵי
נְגִינָה, שֶׁהֵם תִּקּוּן לְהַנַּ"ל.

וְאָז בְּעֵת שֶׁנִּגְלָה הַתּוֹרָה הַנַּ"ל, אָמַר בַּתְּחִלָּה שֶׁתִּקּוּן הָרִאשׁוֹן
הוּא הַמִּקְוֶה, שֶׁצְּרִיכִין לִטְבֹּל בְּמִקְוֶה (וְאָמַר בְּזֶה הַלָּשׁוֹן: דָאס
עֶרְשְׁטֶע אִיז מִקְוֶה); וְאַחַר כָּךְ גִּלָּה הַתִּקּוּן הַנַּ"ל, לוֹמַר עֲשָׂרָה
קַפִּיטְל תְּהִלִּים כַּנַּ"ל. גַּם פַּעַם אַחַת אָמַר שֶׁצָּרִיךְ לִזָּהֵר מְאֹד
לִטְבֹּל בְּאוֹתוֹ הַיּוֹם שֶׁיִּהְיֶה הָאָדָם בִּלְתִּי טָהוֹר, וַאֲפִלּוּ אִם
לֹא יוּכַל לִטְבֹּל בַּבֹּקֶר, עַל כָּל פָּנִים יִטְבֹּל בְּאוֹתוֹ הַיּוֹם, אֲפִלּוּ
לִפְנוֹת עֶרֶב, כִּי צְרִיכִין לִזָּהֵר מְאֹד לִטְבֹּל בְּאוֹתוֹ הַיּוֹם דַּיְקָא
(וְעַיֵּן בְּסוֹף 'סִפּוּרֵי מַעֲשִׂיּוֹת', שֶׁאָמַר שֶׁטּוֹב מְאֹד לִטְבֹּל תֵּכֶף
וּמִיָּד וְכוּ', עַיֵּן שָׁם).

אַחַר כָּךְ אַחַר שֶׁעָבְרוּ קָרוֹב לְאַרְבַּע שָׁנִים, וּמַה שֶּׁעָבַר בְּאֵלּוּ
הַשָּׁנִים יִקְצְרוּ רִבְבוֹת יְרִיעוֹת לְסַפֵּר, וּכְבָר הָיָה לוֹ הַחוֹלַאַת
שֶׁלּוֹ שֶׁנִּסְתַּלֵּק מִמֶּנּוּ, וּכְבָר חָזַר מִלֶּמְבֶּרְג; פַּעַם אַחַת בַּחֹרֶף
שָׁכַב עַל מִטָּתוֹ וַאֲנַחְנוּ עָמַדְנוּ לְפָנָיו, וְהִתְחִיל לְדַבֵּר מֵעִנְיַן
הָעֲשָׂרָה קַפִּיטְל תְּהִלִּים שֶׁהֵם תִּקּוּן לְהַנַּ"ל, וְאָז צִוָּה עָלַי

At this time he did not specify which ten psalms should be said for this remedy. He mentioned that it was indeed desirable that the Ten Psalms should be revealed. But he said that at all events any ten psalms one recites are a remedy, because any group of ten psalms always correspond to the ten forms of song which are the remedy.

When the Rebbe revealed this teaching he started by saying that the first remedy is to immerse in a *mikveh*. ("*Dos ershte iz mikveh*"). It was after that that he revealed the remedy of reciting ten psalms. On another occasion he said one should be careful to immerse on the very same day one is impure. If it is impossible to immerse in the morning one should still immerse that day, even towards evening. He also mentioned that it is best to immerse immediately, as soon as possible.

Four long years passed — and what happened would take volumes to describe. The Rebbe contracted the disease which was to take his life, and it was in this period that he made his journey to Lemberg (Lvov). One winter's night he was lying in bed and we were standing around him when he started talking about the remedy of the Ten Psalms. He asked me to take a piece of paper and

לִכְתֹּב עַל הַנְּיָר הַפְּסוּקִים שֶׁמְרֻמָּז בָּהֶם הָעֲשָׂרָה מִינֵי נְגִינָה
שֶׁהֵם תִּקּוּן לְהַנַּ"ל, וְיָשַׁבְתִּי לִכְתֹּב וּמִפִּיו יִקְרָא אֵלָי, וְגִלָּה לִי
הַפְּסוּקִים, וּכְתַבְתִּים עַל הַסֵּפֶר כַּאֲשֶׁר הֵם נִדְפָּסִים (בְּלִקּוּטֵי
תִּנְיָנָא סִימָן צ"ב הַנַּ"ל). וְאָז גִּלָּה דַעְתּוֹ, שֶׁרְצוֹנוֹ לְגַלּוֹת
בִּפְרָטִיּוּת אֵיזוֹ הֵם הָעֲשָׂרָה קַפִּיטְל תְּהִלִּים שֶׁצְּרִיכִין לוֹמַר
בְּאוֹתוֹ הַיּוֹם; וְהָיִינוּ עוֹמְדִים וּמְצַפִּים שֶׁיְּגַלֶּה לָנוּ, וְלֹא זָכִינוּ
מִיָּד, אַחַר כָּךְ נָסַעְנוּ מֵאִתּוֹ.

וְאַחַר כָּךְ הָיִיתִי אֶצְלוֹ בְּאֵיזֶה שַׁבָּת, וְהִזְמִין ה' יִתְבָּרַךְ
שֶׁרָאִיתִי בְּעֵינַי כְּתִיבַת יָדוֹ הַקְּדוֹשָׁה שֶׁכְּבָר רָשַׁם לְעַצְמוֹ
הָעֲשָׂרָה קַפִּיטְל תְּהִלִּים שֶׁצְּרִיכִין לוֹמַר, אַךְ לֹא הָיָה מִדֶּרֶךְ
אֶרֶץ שֶׁאֶקַּח כְּתַב יָדוֹ בְּעַצְמִי בְּלִי רְשׁוּתוֹ, וְרָצִיתִי לְתָפְּסָם
בְּמֹחִי בְּעַל פֶּה, וְלֹא יָכֹלְתִּי מֵחֲמַת אֵימַת רַבִּי פֶּן יַקְפִּיד,
כִּי בָאתִי לְחַדְרוֹ וּמְצָאתִי כְּתִיבַת יָדוֹ הַנַּ"ל וְהִסְתַּכַּלְתִּי בּוֹ
בְּלֹא רְשׁוּתוֹ (כִּי הַמַּעֲשֶׂה הַזֹּאת הָיָה בְּשַׁבָּת פָּרָשַׁת שְׁקָלִים
שְׁנַת תק"ע, שֶׁהוּא ז"ל יָצָא מֵחַדְרוֹ וְנִכְנַס לַבַּיִת הַגָּדוֹל שֶׁלּוֹ
בְּעֵת קְרִיאַת הַתּוֹרָה, וְאָז נִכְנַסְתִּי בְּחַדְרוֹ וְרָאִיתִי כְּתִיבַת יָדוֹ
הַנַּ"ל).

וְאַחַר כָּךְ, בְּיוֹם רִאשׁוֹן, בְּעֵת שֶׁלָּקַחְתִּי רְשׁוּת מֵאִתּוֹ לָשׁוּב
לְבֵיתִי, דִּבַּרְתִּי עִמּוֹ וְשָׁאַלְתִּי מִמֶּנּוּ שֶׁיְּגַלֶּה לִי עֲשָׂרָה קַפִּיטְל
הַנַּ"ל, כִּי יָדַעְתִּי שֶׁכְּבָר הֵם נִרְשָׁמִים אֶצְלוֹ כַּנַּ"ל; וְלֹא רָצָה,
וְאָמַר שֶׁיִּהְיֶה עֵת אַחַר לָזֶה, וְהָלַכְתִּי מֵאִתּוֹ.

write down the biblical verses which contain references to the ten forms of song which make up the remedy. (The ten verses are revealed in Likutey Moharan II:92.) The Rebbe then said he would like to reveal which are the Ten Psalms themselves. We stood and waited for him to tell us. But we were not worthy of hearing them that time. Then we had to leave.

When I returned for a Shabbat, I happened to see a manuscript in which the Rebbe himself had written down the Ten Psalms. I did not think it proper to take the manuscript without permission. I attempted to memorize it, but was prevented by the fear that the Rebbe would mind my entering the room and seeing the manuscript without his permission. This took place on Shabbat Shekalim 5570/1810 (March 3, 1810). When the Rebbe left his room to hear the reading of the Torah, I entered and saw the manuscript.

On Sunday when I went to take leave of the Rebbe before going home I asked him to reveal to me the Ten Psalms, knowing they were already written down on his list. But he did not want to, and he said there would be another occasion for this.

אַחַר כָּךְ סָמוּךְ לְאוֹתוֹ הָעֵת, בְּעֵת שֶׁהָיִיתִי אֲנִי בְּבֵיתִי
בְּנֶעֶמִירוֹב, אָז גִּלָּה הָעֲשָׂרָה קַפִּיטְל תְּהִלִּים לִפְנֵי הָרַב דְּפֹה
בְּרֶסְלֶב וְלִפְנֵי חֲבֵרֵי רַבִּי נַפְתָּלִי מִנֶּעֶמִירוֹב, וְיִחֵד אוֹתָם לְעֵדוּת
עַל זֶה; וְכָךְ אָמַר לָהֶם: הֱיוֹת בְּעִנְיָן זֶה הַיָּדוּעַ (הַיְנוּ עִנְיַן מִקְרֶה
לַיְלָה חַס וְשָׁלוֹם) נִלְכָּדִים בְּוַדַּאי שְׁלֹשָׁה חֶלְקֵי הָעוֹלָם, אֲנִי
לוֹקֵחַ אֶתְכֶם לְעֵדוּת, וְתֵדְעוּ, שֶׁאֵלּוּ הָעֲשָׂרָה קַפִּיטְל תְּהִלִּים
מוֹעִילִים מְאֹד מְאֹד לְתִקּוּן קֶרִי, וְהֵם תִּקּוּן גָּמוּר וּמוֹעִיל
מְאֹד מְאֹד. וְיֵשׁ מִי שֶׁיִּקְרֶה לוֹ עַל־יְדֵי רִבּוּי אֲכִילָה וּשְׁתִיָּה,
אוֹ עַל־יְדֵי חֲלָשׁוּת וַעֲיֵפוּת, אוֹ עַל־יְדֵי שֶׁאֵינוֹ שׁוֹכֵב כָּרָאוּי,
וְכָל זֶה אֵינוֹ כְלוּם (וְהוּא כְּמוֹ תִינוֹק שֶׁמַּשְׁתִּין בַּשֵּׁנָה). גַּם
יֵשׁ שֶׁשּׁוֹמְרִים אוֹתוֹ מִלְמַעְלָה וְנִצּוֹל מִן הַמִּקְרֶה, אוֹ שֶׁהַמַּזָּל
שׁוֹמֵר אוֹתוֹ וְנִצּוֹל; גַּם לִפְעָמִים נִדְמֶה לְהָאָדָם בַּשֵּׁנָה בַּחֲלוֹם
כְּאִלּוּ הוּא נָפַל וְאַחַר כָּךְ מִתְעוֹרֵר מִשְּׁנָתוֹ, גַּם זֶה מִן הַשָּׁמַיִם
שֶׁמַּצִּילִין אוֹתוֹ מִזֶּה.

רַק מִי שֶׁיִּקְרֶה לוֹ חַס וְשָׁלוֹם מֵחֲמַת הִרְהוּרִים, מִזֶּה נִבְרָאִים
מַמָּשׁ קְלִפּוֹת חַס וְשָׁלוֹם כַּמְבֹאָר בַּסְּפָרִים; אֲבָל מִי שֶׁיֹּאמַר
בְּאוֹתוֹ הַיּוֹם אֵלּוּ הָעֲשָׂרָה קַפִּיטְל תְּהִלִּים בְּוַדַּאי יִתַּקֵּן בָּזֶה
מְאֹד מְאֹד:

וְכַמָּה וְכַמָּה צַדִּיקִים גְּדוֹלִים שֶׁרָצוּ לַעֲמֹד עַל עִנְיָן זֶה וְנִתְיַגְּעוּ
לִמְצֹא לָזֶה תִּקּוּן גָּמוּר, וּקְצָתָם לֹא יָדְעוּ כְּלָל מַהוּ עִנְיָן זֶה,
וּקְצָתָם הִתְחִילוּ לֵידַע קְצָת בְּעִנְיַן תִּקּוּן זֶה, וְנִסְתַּלְּקוּ לְעוֹלָמָם

Not long afterwards, when I was at home in Nemirov, the Rebbe revealed the Ten Psalms to the Rabbi of Breslov and my close friend Rabbi Naftali of Nemirov. He said to them: **"Three quarters of the world are caught in this trap. Now I am going to make you witnesses of my words. Know that these Ten Psalms are highly effective in the case of nocturnal pollutions. In fact they are a complete remedy, and they help very greatly.** There are people who suffer this experience because of eating or drinking too much, or through weakness and over-tiredness, or because they were not lying in a good position. In cases like this it has no significance at all – it is like a child who wets his bed while he is asleep. There are also people who are protected from Above and saved from the pollution, or else their *mazal* – their destiny – protects them and they are saved. At times when a person is asleep he dreams that he is falling and then afterwards he wakes up. This is also because he is protected by Heaven.

"But when a pollution occurs to a person who has been entertaining thoughts and fantasies during the day it really does cause *kelipot* to be created, as is explained in the mystical literature. However if one recites these Ten Psalms on the same day, it is certainly a very powerful remedy.

"Many great Tzadikim wanted to do something about this problem and made great efforts to find a complete remedy for it. Some of them did not understand

בְּאֶמְצַע עָסְקָם בָּזֶה, וְלֹא גָמְרוּ; וְלִי עָזַר ה' יִתְבָּרַךְ שֶׁזָּכִיתִי לַעֲמֹד עַל זֶה בִּשְׁלֵמוּת. וְעִנְיַן תִּקּוּן זֶה עַל־יְדֵי אֲמִירַת הָעֲשָׂרָה קַפִּיטְל תְּהִלִּים הַנַּ"ל הוּא דָּבָר חָדָשׁ לְגַמְרֵי, חִדּוּשׁ נִפְלָא, כִּי הוּא תִּקּוּן נִפְלָא וְנוֹרָא מְאֹד מְאֹד (עַיֵּן לְמַטָּה).

וּמִי שֶׁיּוּכַל לֵילֵךְ לְמִקְוֶה וְאַחַר כָּךְ יֹאמְרֵם – בְּוַדַּאי מַה טּוֹב, אַךְ אֲפִלּוּ אִם הוּא אָנוּס שֶׁאִי אֶפְשָׁר לְטַבֵּל, כְּגוֹן שֶׁהוּא חוֹלֶה אוֹ בַדֶּרֶךְ, אַף־עַל־פִּי־כֵן אִם יֹאמְרֵם אַשְׁרֵי לוֹ, כִּי הֵם תִּקּוּן גָּדוֹל וְנוֹרָא מְאֹד. וְאִם יֹאמְרֵם בְּכַוָּנָה כָּרָאוּי – בְּוַדַּאי מַה טּוֹב, אַךְ גַּם הָאֲמִירָה בְּעַצְמָהּ מְסֻגָּל מְאֹד.

וְאָמַר: כִּי לֹא נוֹדַע זֹאת מִיּוֹם בְּרִיאַת הָעוֹלָם; מִסְּתָמָא הָיִיתִי רוֹצֶה לְבַטֵּל זֹאת לְגַמְרֵי, אַךְ אִי אֶפְשָׁר זֹאת, לֹא בְּגַשְׁמִיּוּת וְלֹא בְּרוּחָנִיּוּת: בְּגַשְׁמִיּוּת אִי אֶפְשָׁר, כִּי הָיָה צָרִיךְ לְבַטֵּל וּלְשַׁנּוֹת הַטֶּבַע שֶׁל כְּלָלִיּוּת בְּנֵי אָדָם בִּתְמִידוּת, וְזֶה דָּבָר שֶׁאִי אֶפְשָׁר, כִּי אֲפִלּוּ מֹשֶׁה רַבֵּנוּ עָלָיו הַשָּׁלוֹם, וְכַיּוֹצֵא, שֶׁבִּטְּלוּ הַטֶּבַע, הָיָה רַק לְפִי שָׁעָה וּבְדָבָר פְּרָטִי, כְּגוֹן קְרִיעַת יַם סוּף אוֹ בְּקִיעַת הַיַּרְדֵּן וְכַיּוֹצֵא, שֶׁהָיָה רַק לְפִי שָׁעָה, אֲבָל לְבַטֵּל הַטֶּבַע שֶׁל כְּלָלִיּוּת בְּנֵי אָדָם, כִּי כָּל אֶחָד וְאֶחָד, בְּהֶכְרֵחַ לְבַטֵּל וּלְשַׁנּוֹת הַטֶּבַע אֶצְלוֹ, וְגַם צָרִיךְ לְבַטֵּל וּלְשַׁנּוֹת

what is involved at all. Others began to understand somewhat and get a glimmer of the remedy, however they were taken from this world in the middle of their labors and they never completed the task. But God has helped me, and I have been worthy of complete success. This remedy of reciting the Ten Psalms is completely original. It is a remarkable contribution, because the remedy is wonderful, indeed awesome.

"If one can go to the *mikveh* and afterwards recite these Psalms, it is excellent. Even if he is unavoidably prevented from immersing, through sickness for example, or because he is on a journey, even so, if he recites the Ten Psalms, "Happy is he," because they are a great and awesome remedy. If he says them with understanding and devotion, this is certainly very good. But even simply saying the words is very effective.

"This remedy has not been discovered since the world was created. I would have liked to do away with this problem completely, but that is simply not possible, either on the physical or the spiritual levels. Physically it is impossible because it would be necessary to change the nature of the entire human race for all time. Such a thing is impossible. Even when Moses and other outstanding Tzadikim suspended nature, it was only a temporary measure for a particular purpose, such as the splitting of the Red Sea or the River Jordan, which only took place for a limited time. But in this case it would be necessary to alter the nature of the entire

הַטֶּבַע תָּמִיד, וְזֶה דָּבָר שֶׁאִי אֶפְשָׁר; וְגַם בְּרוּחָנִיּוּת אִי אֶפְשָׁר
וְכוּ'. אַךְ הָעֲשָׂרָה קַפִּיטְל הֵם דָּבָר נִפְלָא וְיָקָר וּמוֹעִיל מְאֹד.

גַּם יַחַד אוֹתָם לְעֵדוּת, וְאָמַר, שֶׁגַּם כִּי יִמְלְאוּ יָמָיו, אֲזַי אַחַר
הִסְתַּלְּקוּתוֹ, מִי שֶׁיָּבוֹא עַל קִבְרוֹ וְיֹאמַר שָׁם אֵלּוּ הָעֲשָׂרָה
קַפִּיטְל תְּהִלִּים הַנַּ"ל וְיִתֵּן פְּרוּטָה לִצְדָקָה (נוּסָח אַחֵר:
עֲבוּרוֹ), אֲפִלּוּ אִם גָּדְלוּ וְעָצְמוּ עֲוֹנוֹתָיו וַחֲטָאָיו מְאֹד מְאֹד
חַס וְשָׁלוֹם, אֲזַי אֶתְאַמֵּץ וְאֶשְׁתַּדֵּל לָאֹרֶךְ וְלָרֹחַב לְהוֹשִׁיעוֹ
וּלְתַקְּנוֹ וְכוּ', וְאָמַר בְּזֶה הַלָּשׁוֹן: אִיךְ וֶועל מִיךְ לֵייגֶען אִין דֶער
לֶענְג אוּן אִין דֶער בְּרֵייט אִיךְ זָאל אִיהֶם אַ טוֹבָה טְהוּן, בַּיי
דִי פֵּאוֹת וֶועל אִיךְ אִיהֶם אֲרוֹיס צִיהֶן פוּן שְׁאוֹל תַּחְתִּיּוֹת;
וַאֲנִי חָזָק מְאֹד בְּכָל הַדְּבָרִים שֶׁלִּי, אַךְ בָּזֶה אֲנִי חָזָק בְּיוֹתֵר,
שֶׁאֵלּוּ הָעֲשָׂרָה קַפִּיטְל תְּהִלִּים מוֹעִילִים מְאֹד מְאֹד.

וְאֵלּוּ הֵן הָעֲשָׂרָה קַפִּיטְל תְּהִלִּים: טז, לב, מא, מב, נט, עז,
צ, קה, קכ, קנ, כַּאֲשֶׁר כְּבָר נִדְפְּסוּ כַּמָּה פְּעָמִים (רַק בְּסֵפֶר
'סִפּוּרֵי מַעֲשִׂיּוֹת' נִדְפְּסוּ בַּפַּעַם הָרִאשׁוֹן בְּטָעוּת הַקַּפִּיטְל
שֶׁל קל"ז עַל־יְדֵי עֲווּת הַמַּדְפִּיסִים, וּמִשָּׁם נִתְפַּשֵּׁט הַטָּעוּת
בְּכַמָּה סְפָרִים וְסִדּוּרִים שֶׁהֶעְתִּיקוּ מִשָּׁם); וְיֹאמְרֵם כַּסֵּדֶר
שֶׁהֵם כְּתוּבִים בַּתְּהִלִּים.

וְאָמַר שֶׁהוּא תִּקּוּן הַכְּלָלִי; כִּי כָּל עֲבֵרָה יֵשׁ לָהּ תִּקּוּן מְיֻחָד,
אֲבָל תִּקּוּן הַנַּ"ל הוּא תִּקּוּן הַכְּלָלִי. גַּם אָמַר אָז שֶׁעִנְיָן הַנַּ"ל
שֶׁל הָעֲשָׂרָה קַפִּיטְל תְּהִלִּים יֹאמְרוּ וִיגַלּוּ בִּפְנֵי הַכֹּל.

human race, which would mean changing the nature of every single individual – and not merely temporarily but permanently. This would be impossible. On a spiritual level also it would be impossible. But the Ten Psalms are a most precious and effective remedy."

The Rebbe made the Rabbi of Breslov and Rabbi Naftali his witnesses, and said: **"When my days are ended and I leave this world, I will intercede for anyone who comes to my grave, recites these Ten Psalms, and gives to charity. No matter how grave his sins and transgressions, I will do everything in my power to save him and cleanse him. I will span the length and breadth of the creation for him. I'll take hold of his** *peyot* (side-curls) **and pull him out of Gehinnom!"**

"I am very positive in everything I say. But I am more positive about this than about anything when I say that these Psalms help very, very much."

"These are the Ten Psalms: **16, 32, 41, 42, 59, 77, 90, 105, 137, 150**." These Psalms have been published numerous times. [However, in the first edition of Sipurey Ma'asiot, because of a printing error, another Psalm was erroneously substituted for Psalm 137. This error spread to a number of other published works.] They should be recited in this order, which is the order in which they appear in the Book of Psalms.

"This is the Tikkun Klali, the Complete Remedy. Every sin has its own individual remedy. But this is the Complete Remedy." "Go out and spread the teaching of

וְאָמַר: אַף־עַל־פִּי שֶׁהוּא דָּבָר קַל לוֹמַר עֲשָׂרָה קַפִּיטְל תְּהִלִּים, אַף־עַל־פִּי־כֵן גַּם זֶה יִהְיֶה כָּבֵד מְאֹד לְקַיֵּם. וְכֵן נִתְקַיֵּם עַתָּה בַּעֲווֹנוֹתֵינוּ הָרַבִּים, שֶׁמֵּחֲמַת רִבּוּי הַמַּחֲלֹקֶת רַב הֶהָמוֹן רְחוֹקִים לְקַיֵּם זֹאת, וְהוּא ז"ל הוֹדִיעַ כָּל זֹאת מִקֹּדֶם. וַאֲנַחְנוּ עָשִׂינוּ מַה שֶּׁמֻּטָּל עָלֵינוּ – לְהוֹדִיעַ הַתִּקּוּן לְכָל הֶחָפֵץ לְהִתְתַּקֵּן; וְכָל אֶחָד הַטּוֹב בְּעֵינָיו יַעֲשֶׂה, הַשּׁוֹמֵעַ יִשְׁמַע וְהֶחָדֵל יֶחְדָּל, וַאֲנַחְנוּ אֶת נַפְשֵׁנוּ הִצַּלְנוּ.

וּמַה שֶּׁהֶרַב בַּעַל הַמְחַבֵּר 'סֵדֶר תִּקּוּן שַׁבָּת' מְבִיאָם בְּשֵׁם סֵפֶר 'עֲשָׂרָה הִלּוּלִים', זֶה אֵינוֹ, כִּי יְדִידִי הַקּוֹרֵא, עַיֵּן נָא בְּסֵפֶר 'תִּקּוּן מוֹעֵד', וְתִרְאֶה שֶׁמּוּבָאִים שָׁם בְּפֵרוּשׁ בְּשֵׁם רַבֵּנוּ הָרַב רַבִּי נַחְמָן ז"ל; וְכֵן בְּכַמָּה סְפָרִים יֵשׁ שֶׁמּוּבָאִים שָׁם בְּשֵׁם רַבֵּנוּ ז"ל; וְגַם נַס נָא וְחַפֵּשׂ בְּכָל הַסְּפָרִים שֶׁמּוּבָאִים שָׁם שֶׁלֹּא בְשֵׁם רַבֵּנוּ ז"ל, וְתִרְאֶה שֶׁכֻּלָּם נִדְפְּסוּ אַחַר פְּטִירַת רַבֵּנוּ ז"ל, שֶׁנִּפְטַר תְּחִלַּת שְׁנַת תקע"א בְּחֹל הַמּוֹעֵד סֻכּוֹת. וְאֶפְשָׁר שֶׁהֶרַב הַנַּ"ל וְכַיּוֹצֵא, מִגֹּדֶל תְּשׁוּקָתָם לְזַכּוֹת בָּהֶם אֶת הָרַבִּים בְּתִקּוּן גָּדוֹל כָּזֶה, וְיָדוּעַ שֶׁיֵּשׁ שֶׁנִּמְצָאִים מִתְנַגְּדִים וְחוֹלְקִים עַל רַבֵּנוּ ז"ל, עַל כֵּן קִיְּמוּ בְּנַפְשָׁם מַאֲמַר חֲכָמֵינוּ ז"ל (יבמות סה:) שֶׁמֻּתָּר לְשַׁנּוֹת בִּדְבַר הַשָּׁלוֹם, וּבִפְרָט בְּדָבָר גָּדוֹל וְתִקּוּן כָּזֶה.

these Ten Psalms to all men. It may seem like an easy thing to say ten psalms. But in practice it will prove to be very difficult to do so." Owing to our many sins, the Rebbe's last words literally came true. Because of much opposition, most of the world has been prevented from using this remedy. But the Rebbe had already predicted this. We have done our part to teach this remedy to all who wish to find the remedy. Let every man do as he sees fit. Listen if you want to, or ignore it if you will. Our own souls we have saved (Ezekiel 3:19).

The author of Tikkun Shabbat attributes these Ten Psalms to a work called Asarah Hilulim. This is an error. In Tikkun Mo'ed, they are explicitly attributed to "our master, Rebbe Nachman of blessed memory." Many other authors also attribute these Ten Psalms to the Rebbe. If you carefully examine all the works that refer to the Ten Psalms without mentioning the Rebbe's name, you will find that they were all published after his death on Sukkot 5571 (October 16, 1810). Perhaps some authors attributed the Ten Psalms to another source because of the great opposition that the Rebbe suffered. They may have wanted the greatest possible number of people to be able to use the remedy and therefore took advantage of the Talmudic dictum, "It is permissible to alter the truth for the sake of peace" (Yebamot 65b). This is especially true in the case of something as important as this remedy.

וְעַתָּה בֵּין תָּבִין שֶׁצַּדְקוּ הַנֶּאֱמָר לְעֵיל, שֶׁהֵם תִּקּוּן חָדָשׁ לְגַמְרֵי וְלֹא יָדַע מִזֶּה שׁוּם נִבְרָא מִימוֹת עוֹלָם. וְתֹאמְרֵם בְּשֵׁם רַבֵּנוּ ז"ל, בִּכְדֵי שֶׁשִּׂפְתוֹתָיו יִהְיוּ דּוֹבְבוֹת וְכוּ' (סנהדרין צ:), אֲשֶׁר כָּל הַצַּדִּיקִים מִתְגַּעְגְּעִים לָזֶה; וּמִזֶּה אֲשֶׁר אִלְצוּנִי לְגַלּוֹת כָּל הַנַּ"ל. וּזְכוּתוֹ יַעֲמֹד לָנוּ, וּמִכָּל פְּגָמֵינוּ וְצָרוֹתֵינוּ יְתַקְּנֵנוּ וְיוֹשִׁיעֵנוּ, אָמֵן כֵּן יְהִי רָצוֹן.

וּמְבֹאָר גַּם בְּהַשִּׂיחוֹת שֶׁאַחַר הַסִּפּוּרֵי מַעֲשִׂיּוֹת, שֶׁהִזְהִיר לַאֲנָשָׁיו, שֶׁכְּשֶׁיִּקְרָה לָהֶם מִקְרֶה בִּלְתִּי טָהוֹר חַס וְשָׁלוֹם, שֶׁיֵּלְכוּ תֵּכֶף וּמִיָּד לְמִקְוֶה לִטְבֹּל, כִּי עַל־יְדֵי הַמִּקְרֶה חַס וְשָׁלוֹם נַעֲשָׂה מַה שֶׁנַּעֲשָׂה, עַל כֵּן טוֹב מְאֹד שֶׁקֹּדֶם שֶׁמַּתְחִיל לְהַעֲשׂוֹת מִזֶּה אֵיזֶה דָבָר חַס וְשָׁלוֹם, שֶׁיַּקְדִּים עַצְמוֹ הָאָדָם וְיִטְבֹּל וִיטַהֵר עַצְמוֹ.

וְהִזְהִיר מְאֹד לְבַל יִתְפַּחֵד הָאָדָם מִזֶּה כְּלָל, כִּי הַפַּחַד וְהַדְּאָגוֹת וְהַמָּרָה שְׁחוֹרוֹת בְּעִנְיָן זֶה מַזִּיק מְאֹד מְאֹד. בִּפְרָט אַחַר שֶׁגִּלָּה אֵלּוּ הָעֲשָׂרָה קַפִּיטְל תְּהִלִּים הַנַּ"ל הַמְסֻגָּלִים לְתִקּוּן חֵטְא זֶה, אָז אָמַר, שֶׁמִּי שֶׁיִּזְכֶּה לְקַיֵּם זֹאת לוֹמַר אֵלּוּ הָעֲשָׂרָה קַפִּיטְל תְּהִלִּים הַנַּ"ל, בְּאוֹתוֹ הַיּוֹם שֶׁיִּקְרֶה לוֹ חַס וְשָׁלוֹם, אֲזַי בְּוַדַּאי יְתֻקַּן חֶטְאוֹ, וְשׁוּב אַל יִדְאַג כְּלָל.

גַּם הָיָה מִתְלוֹצֵץ מֵאֵלּוּ הַחֲסִידִים וְהַיְרֵאִים, שֶׁכְּשֶׁמַּגִּיעַ לָהֶם אֵיזֶה הִרְהוּר, אֲזַי הֵם מִתְפַּחֲדִים שֶׁלֹּא יָבוֹאוּ לִידֵי מִקְרֶה,

But we have already mentioned that this is an absolutely new remedy and was never revealed since the beginning of time. Say these Ten Psalms in the name of the Rebbe so that his lips should murmur them (Sanhedrin 90b), which is something all tzaddikim desire.

This is what motivated me to disclose all this. May the Rebbe's merit stand up for us; may he rectify all our sins and suffering and save us. Amen, may it be God's will.

(Rebbe Nachman's Wisdom #141)

Rabbi Noson continues: The Rebbe told his followers that whenever they experienced a nocturnal emission, they should immediately immerse in a mikvah. As a result of this nocturnal pollution, whatever damage was done, was done. However, before a permanent impression is made, one should immerse and purify oneself.

The Rebbe warned that one should not be frightened by this at all. Fear, worry, and depression are very harmful as far as this is concerned. This is especially true now that he has revealed the Ten Psalms that have the specific power to rectify this sin. If a person recites these ten psalms on the day that he has had a nocturnal emission, his sin is rectified, and he need not have any further concern.

The Rebbe laughed at Chasidim and God-fearing men who were terrified whenever they had an untoward thought, lest they experience a nocturnal pollution.

וּמֵחֲמַת זֶה הֵם רְגִילִים בְּהֶתֵּר – מֵחֲמַת פַּחַד שֶׁלֹּא יָבֹואוּ לִידֵי מִקְרֶה, וְהוּא ז"ל הָיָה מִתְלֹוצֵץ מִזֶּה. וְעִקַּר כַּוָּנָתֹו הָיָה, שֶׁהָאָדָם צָרִיךְ לְבִלְי לְהִתְפַּחֵד וּלְהִתְיָרֵא כְּלָל מִדְּבָרִים כָּאֵלּוּ, וְלִבְלִי לַחֲשֹׁב מַחֲשָׁבֹות כְּלָל בְּעִנְיָן זֶה, רַק יִהְיֶה כְּגִבֹּור חַיִל לַעֲמֹד כְּנֶגֶד תַּאֲוָתֹו וְיָסִיחַ דַּעְתֹּו מִזֶּה לְגַמְרֵי, וְאַל יִתְפַּחֵד כְּלָל, וַה' הַטֹּוב בְּעֵינָיו יַעֲשֶׂה עִמֹּו מַה שֶׁהוּא יִתְבָּרַךְ חָפֵץ.

וְרָמַז בִּדְבָרָיו שֶׁזֶּה הָיָה בְּחִינַת פְּגַם שֶׁל דָּוִד הַמֶּלֶךְ עָלָיו הַשָּׁלֹום בְּבַת שֶׁבַע וְכוּ', וְלֹא בֵּאֵר הַדָּבָר הֵיטֵב: וּמְאֹד מְאֹד צְרִיכִין לְהִתְחַזֵּק בְּשִׂמְחָה תָּמִיד, וְאַל יִפֹּל בְּדַעְתֹּו כְּלָל מִשֹּׁום דָּבָר שֶׁבָּעֹולָם – אַף אִם יַעֲבֹר עָלָיו מָה. וְאִם יִהְיֶה חָזָק בְּדַעְתֹּו וְלֹא יִתְפַּחֵד כְּלָל וְלֹא יַחֲשֹׁב מַחֲשָׁבֹות כְּלָל (שֶׁקֹּורִין אִיבֶּער טְרַאכְטִין) וְיֵלֵךְ בְּתֻמֹּו בְּשִׂמְחָה, יִזְכֶּה לַסֹּוף לַעֲבֹר עַל הַכֹּל בְּשָׁלֹום. וּדְבָרִים כָּאֵלּוּ אִי אֶפְשָׁר לְבָאֵר בִּכְתָב, וְעָרֹום יָבִין לְאַשּׁוּרֹו:

גַּם בְּלֹא זֶה הִזְהִיר מְאֹד לִהְיֹות רָגִיל בִּטְבִילַת מִקְוֶה, וְאָמַר שֶׁבַּיָּמִים שֶׁאֵין אֹומְרִים 'תַּחֲנוּן', כְּגֹון בְּיֹומֵי דְנִיסָן וְכַיֹּוצֵא, הַמּוּבָאִים בְּשֻׁלְחָן עָרוּךְ אֹרַח חַיִּים, צְרִיכִין לִהְיֹות רָגִיל בְּיֹותֵר בִּטְבִילַת מִקְוֶה (שִׂיחֹות הָר"ן סִימָן קכה). כֵּן נִזְכֶּה לְקַיֵּם כָּל דְּבָרָיו בֶּאֱמֶת וּבְתָמִים, אָמֵן כֵּן יְהִי רָצֹון:

■ ■ ■

However, the fear itself can often bring that which they wished to avoid. He therefore mocked this. His main teaching was that a person not be afraid or terrified by this. One should not think about it at all. One should be like a mighty warrior, standing up against one's desires, utterly fearless, and not thinking of them at all. Then, "God will do what is good in His eyes" (Samuel I 3:18), as He desires.

In his discussion, Rebbe Nachman hinted that this was the blemish of King David and Batsheva... However, he did not explain this very clearly. However, a man must strengthen himself in joy at all times, and not let anything depress him, no matter what happens. If he is strong in his resolve, he will not be afraid at all, and will not dwell upon such thoughts. He will travel in his ample way with joy, and he will overcome everything in peace. It is impossible to put such words into writing. However, "a prudent man will follow the right path" (Proverbs 14:15). *(Rebbe Nachman's Stories pp. 455-6)*

In any event, Rebbe Nachman had already stated to be very careful to frequently immerse in the mikvah, especially on those days associated with festivity when *Tachanun*, the penitential prayer, is not said. Then one must be extra careful to immerse *(see Rebbe Nachman's Wisdom #185)*.

May we merit fulfilling all of his words in true honesty and simplicity, Amen, may it be His Will.

▪ ▪ ▪

אָמַר הַמַּעְתִּיק: כְּתִיב (משלי כה, יא): "תַּפּוּחֵי זָהָב
בְּמַשְׂכִּיּוֹת כָּסֶף דָּבָר דָּבֻר עַל אָפְנָיו", לָכֵן אָמַרְתִּי לְהַצִּיג פֹּה
מְעַט מִזְּעֵיר מִמַּאַמְרֵי חַכְמֵינוּ ז"ל אֲשֶׁר שָׁם מְבֹאַר גֹּדֶל זְכוּת
הַצַּדִּיקִים אַחַר הִסְתַּלְּקוּתָם לְמַעְלָה לְמַעְלָה, וְכַמָּה גָּדוֹל
הַזְּכוּת וְהַתּוֹעֶלֶת שֶׁל הַמְהַלְּכִים עַל קִבְרָם הַקָּדוֹשׁ זְכוּתָם יָגֵן
עָלֵינוּ, אָמֵן כֵּן יְהִי רָצוֹן:

בְּמִדְרָשׁ רַבָּה פָּרָשַׁת כִּי תִשָּׂא פָּרָשָׁה מ"ד, עַל פָּסוּק 'זְכֹר
לְאַבְרָהָם' וְכוּ' (שמות לב, יג) – הֲדָא הוּא דִכְתִיב (תהלים פ,
ט): "גֶּפֶן מִמִּצְרַיִם תַּסִּיעַ" וְכוּ' וְכוּ', וּלְבַסּוֹף מוּבָא בְּזֶה הַלָּשׁוֹן:
מָה הַגֶּפֶן הִיא חַיָּה וְנִשְׁעֶנֶת עַל עֵצִים מֵתִים, כָּךְ יִשְׂרָאֵל הֵם
חַיִּים וְקַיָּמִים וְנִשְׁעָנִים עַל הַמֵּתִים – אֵלּוּ הָאָבוֹת. וְכֵן אַתָּה
מוֹצֵא כַּמָּה תְפִלּוֹת הִתְפַּלֵּל אֵלִיָּהוּ בְּהַר הַכַּרְמֶל שֶׁתֵּרֵד הָאֵשׁ,
כְּמָה דְאַתְּ אָמַר: "עֲנֵנִי ה' עֲנֵנִי" (מלכים־א יח, לז) – וְלֹא
נַעֲנָה, אֶלָּא כֵּיוָן שֶׁהִזְכִּיר אֶת הַמֵּתִים, וְאָמַר: "ה' אֱלֹהֵי
אַבְרָהָם יִצְחָק וְיִשְׂרָאֵל" (שם, לו) – מִיָּד נַעֲנָה, מַה כְּתִיב
(שם, לח): "וַתִּפֹּל אֵשׁ ה'". וְכֵן מֹשֶׁה, בְּשָׁעָה שֶׁעָשׂוּ יִשְׂרָאֵל
אוֹתוֹ מַעֲשֶׂה, עָמַד וְלִמֵּד עֲלֵיהֶם זְכוּת אַרְבָּעִים יוֹם וְאַרְבָּעִים
לַיְלָה – וְלֹא נַעֲנָה, אֶלָּא כֵּיוָן שֶׁהִזְכִּיר אֶת הַמֵּתִים – מִיָּד
נַעֲנָה, שֶׁנֶּאֱמַר (שמות לב, יג): "זְכֹר לְאַבְרָהָם לְיִצְחָק
וּלְיִשְׂרָאֵל", מַה כְּתִיב: "וַיִּנָּחֶם ה' עַל הָרָעָה" (שמות לב, יד),

> *Here is a selection of some of the many comments of our sages of blessed memory about the great merit of the Tzadikim in the worlds above after their death, and the great benefit of visiting their holy graves. May their merits protect us. Amen.*

The Midrash Rabbah (*Ki Tissa* 44, on the verse "Remember Abraham..." quotes Ps. 80:9 "Thou didst pluck up a vine out of Egypt") and comments: "Just like the vine lives by being supported on the wood of dead trees, so Israel lives and endures through being supported by the dead – namely the Patriarchs. We find that Eliyahu prayed many prayers on Mt. Carmel in order for the fire to descend – 'Answer me, Lord, answer me', but he was only answered because he made mention of the deceased, and said, 'Lord God of Abraham, Isaac and Israel'. When he did so, he was answered immediately: 'Then the fire of Hashem fell' (Kings I 18:36-38). So it was when the Children of Israel committed the sin of the Golden Calf. Moses rose and defended them for forty days and forty nights, but he was only answered when he made mention of the deceased, as it is said, 'Remember Abraham, Isaac and Israel.' What does the Torah go on to say? 'And Hashem repented of the evil which He said He would do unto His people.' (Ex.

הֱוֵי: כְּשֵׁם שֶׁהַגֶּפֶן הַזֹּאת חַיָּה וְנִשְׁעֶנֶת עַל עֵצִים מֵתִים, כָּךְ יִשְׂרָאֵל חַיִּים וְנִשְׁעָנִים עַל הָאָבוֹת כְּשֶׁהֵם מֵתִים, הֱוֵי: "זְכֹר לְאַבְרָהָם לְיִצְחָק וּלְיִשְׂרָאֵל" וְכוּ':

וּבַזֹּהַר הַקָּדוֹשׁ פָּרָשַׁת אַחֲרֵי דַּף ע"א עַמּוּד א' וְ-ב' מוּבָא שָׁם דְּבָרִים נִפְלָאִים וְנוֹרָאִים מִזֶּה הָעִנְיָן הַקָּדוֹשׁ, וְזֶה: תָּאנָא, אָמַר רַבִּי יְהוּדָה, יוֹמָא חַד הֲווֹ אַזְלֵי רַבִּי חִזְקִיָּה וְרַבִּי יֵיסָא בְּאוֹרְחָא, עָרְעוּ בְּגוּשׁ חָלָב וַהֲוָה חָרִיב, יָתְבוּ סָמוּךְ לְבֵי קִבְרֵי וְכוּ', עַיֵּן שָׁם הַמַּעֲשֶׂה הַנִּפְלָאָה. וּבְסוֹף אִיתָא בְּזֶה הַלָּשׁוֹן: אָמְרֵי, וַדַּאי בְּשַׁעְתָּא דְּזַכָּאִין לָא אִשְׁתְּכָחוּ בְּעָלְמָא, עָלְמָא לָא מִתְקַיְּמָא אֶלָּא בְּגִינַיְהוּ דִּמְתַיָּא. אָמַר רַבִּי יֵיסָא: בְּשַׁעְתָּא דְּאִצְטְרִיךְ עָלְמָא לְמִטְרָא, אַמַּאי אַזְלִינָן לְגַבַּיְהוּ דִּמְתַיָּא, וְהָא כְּתִיב (דברים יח, יא) 'וְדֹרֵשׁ אֶל הַמֵּתִים' – וְאָסִיר, אָמַר לֵהּ: עַד כְּעַן לָא חֲמֵיתָא גַּדְפָּא דְצִפֳּרָא דְּעֵדֶן, 'וְדֹרֵשׁ אֶל הַמֵּתִים' – אֶל הַמֵּתִים דַּיְקָא, דְּאִנּוּן חַיָּבֵי עָלְמָא וְכוּ' – דְּאִשְׁתְּכָחוּ תָּדִיר מֵתִים, אֲבָל יִשְׂרָאֵל דְּאִנּוּן זַכָּאֵי קְשׁוֹט, שְׁלֹמֹה קָרָא עֲלַיְהוּ (קהלת ד, ב) 'וְשַׁבֵּחַ אֲנִי אֶת הַמֵּתִים שֶׁכְּבָר מֵתוּ' – בְּזִמְנָא אַחֲרָא וְלָא הַשָּׁתָּא, 'שֶׁכְּבָר מֵתוּ' – וְהַשָּׁתָּא אִנּוּן חַיִּין.

וְעוֹד, דִּשְׁאָר עַמִּין, כַּד אָתוּ לְמֵתֵיהוֹן אַתְיָן בְּחַרְשִׁין לְאִתְעֲרָא עֲלַיְהוּ זִינִין בִּישִׁין, וְכַד יִשְׂרָאֵל אַתְיָן לְמֵתֵיהוֹן, אַתְיָן בְּכַמָּה תְּשׁוּבָה לְקַמֵּי קֻדְשָׁא בְּרִיךְ הוּא, בִּתְבִירוּ דְלִבָּא, בְּתַעֲנִיתָא לְקַבְּלֵהּ, וְכֹלָּא בְּגִין דְּנִשְׁמָתִין קַדִּישִׁין יִבְעוֹן רַחֲמֵי לְקַמֵּי

32:13,14). Just like the vine lives by being supported on dead trees, so Israel lives and is supported by the dead Patriarchs. 'Remember Abraham, Isaac and Israel' etc.."

In the Holy Zohar there is an extraordinary passage dealing with this subject (Zohar III, 70b) – Rabbi Yehuda said: "One day Chizkiah and R. Yaissa were going together when they came to Gush Chalav, which they found in ruins. They sat down near the graveyard, etc." (*See the whole passage.*) The passage ends with the following words: "They said, 'Indeed, at a time when no righteous are found in the world, the world is only sustained through the merit of the dead.' R. Yaissa asked, 'When the world is in need of rain why do we go to the graves of the dead. Is it not written that it is "forbidden to inquire of the dead" (Deut. 18:11)' He replied, 'So far you have not seen the wing of the bird of Eden (a reference to R. Shimon bar Yochai). When the Torah speaks of not enquiring of the "dead", it is speaking of those who truly are dead – the sinners. They are dead forever. But Israel are truly worthy, and King Solomon said of them: "I praise the dead who have already died" (Ecclesiastes 4:2) – they were dead previously, but not now. Before they were deceased, but now they are alive.

Furthermore, when the other nations go to visit their dead, they go with spells to summon evil spirits. But when Israel go to visit their dead, they go in the spirit of repentance before the Holy One, blessed-be-He. Then the Holy One takes pity on the world for their

קֻדְשָׁא בְּרִיךְ הוּא עֲלַיְהוּ, וְקֻדְשָׁא בְּרִיךְ הוּא חָיֵּיס עַל עָלְמָא
בְּגִינַיְהוּ. וְעַל דָּא תְּנֵינָן: צַדִּיקַיָּא, אַף־עַל־גַּב דְּאִתְפְּטַר מֵהַאי
עָלְמָא, לָא אִסְתַּלַּק וְלָא אִתְאֲבִיד מִכֻּלְּהוּ עָלְמִין, דְּהָא בְּכֻלְּהוּ
עָלְמִין אִשְׁתְּכַח יַתִּיר מֵחַיּוֹי, דִּבְחַיּוֹי אִשְׁתְּכַח בְּהַאי עָלְמָא
בִּלְחוֹדוֹי, וּלְבָתַר אִשְׁתְּכַח בִּתְלַת עָלְמִין, וְזַמִּין לְגַבַּיְהוּ, דִּכְתִיב
(שִׁיר־הַשִּׁירִים א, ג): "עֲלָמוֹת אֲהֵבוּךָ" – אַל תִּקְרֵי 'עֲלָמוֹת'
אֶלָּא 'עוֹלָמוֹת', זַכָּאָה חוּלָקֵיהוֹן. תָּאנָא, כְּתִיב (שְׁמוּאֵל־א
כה, כט): "וְהָיְתָה נֶפֶשׁ אֲדֹנִי צְרוּרָה בִּצְרוֹר הַחַיִּים", 'וְהָיְתָה
נֶפֶשׁ אֲדֹנִי', נִשְׁמַת אֲדֹנִי מִבְּעֵי לֵהּ. אֶלָּא כְּמָה דַּאֲמָרָן, דְּזַכָּאָה
חוּלָקֵיהוֹן דְּצַדִּיקַיָּא, דְּכֹלָּא אִתְקְשַׁר דָּא בְּדָא, נֶפֶשׁ בְּרוּחַ,
וְרוּחַ בִּנְשָׁמָה, וּנְשָׁמָה בְּקֻדְשָׁא בְּרִיךְ הוּא, אִשְׁתְּכַח דְּנֶפֶשׁ
צְרוּרָה בִּצְרוֹר הַחַיִּים, עַד כָּאן לִשׁוֹנוֹ הַקָּדוֹשׁ. וְעוֹד מוּבָא
בְּהַפֵּרוּשׁ שֶׁל הָעֵין יַעֲקֹב וְזֶה לְשׁוֹנוֹ: 'שֶׁכְּבָר מֵתוּ' – בְּפוּלְחָנָא
דְּמָארֵיהוֹן:

מִכָּל הַמַּאֲמָרִים הַקְּדוֹשִׁים הַנַּ"ל רוֹאִין גֹּדֶל יְקָרַת זְכוּת
הַצַּדִּיקִים אֲשֶׁר כְּבָר הָלְכוּ לְעוֹלָמָם, אַשְׁרֵי הָאִישׁ אֲשֶׁר
יִסְמֹךְ עַל זְכוּתָם כָּל יְמֵי חַיָּיו וְלֹא יִתְיָאֵשׁ אֶת עַצְמוֹ מִן
הָרַחֲמִים לְעוֹלָם, וּבְכָל מַה שֶּׁיַּעֲבֹר עָלָיו כָּל יְמֵי חַיָּיו, הֵן
בְּרוּחָנִיּוּת וְהֵן בְּגַשְׁמִיּוּת, יִסְמֹךְ עַל זְכוּתָם, וְיִשָּׂא יָדָיו וְלִבּוֹ
לָאֵל אֱמוּנָה יִתְבָּרַךְ, וּבְוַדַּאי יוֹשַׁע; כָּל שֶׁכֵּן "לִקְדוֹשִׁים אֲשֶׁר
בָּאָרֶץ הֵמָּה וְאַדִּירֵי כָּל חֶפְצִי בָם", וּבִפְרָט כְּשֶׁהוֹלְכִין עַל

sakes. We have learned that even when the *Tzadik* passes from this world, he does not really disappear from any world, because he is to be found in all the worlds more than in his lifetime. In his lifetime he was only to be found in this world. But afterwards he is to be found in three worlds. This world, *Nefesh* – Lower Eden, *Ruach* – Upper Eden, *Neshama*. Thus it is written, "Therefore do the maidens (*alamot*) love thee." (Song of Songs 3) Do not read maidens (*alamot*) but worlds (*olamot*). Happy is their portion! Thus we find that Abigail said to David: "May the soul (*nefesh*) of my lord be bound in the bundle of life" (Sam. I, 25:29). Instead of speaking of his *nefesh*, which refers to the lowest part of the soul, we might have expected her to have mentioned his *Neshama*, the highest part of the soul. But happy is the portion of the *Tzadikim*, for each is bound up with the other, the *nefesh* with the *ruach*, the *ruach* with the *neshama* and the *neshama* with the Holy One, blessed-be-He.

From these various passages it is possible to see how precious is the merit of the *Tzadikim* who have already passed on. Happy is the man who relies on their merits all the days of his life and never despairs of receiving God's love. Regardless of what he may endure throughout his days, whether spiritually or physically, he relies on their merits and lifts his hands and his heart to the faithful God, knowing that He will certainly send help, as it is written: "As for the holy ones that are in the earth, they are the excellent ones in whom is all my delight"

קִבְרֵיהֶם הַקְּדוֹשִׁים, כַּמּוּבָן מִפֵּרוּשׁ רַשִׁ"י בְּפָרָשַׁת 'שְׁלַח לְךָ'
עַל פָּסוּק "וַיָּבֹא עַד חֶבְרוֹן" (במדבר יג, כב), וּפֵרֵשׁ רַשִׁ"י –
וְהוּא מַאֲמַר חֲכָמֵינוּ זַ"ל, שֶׁכָּלֵב לְבַדּוֹ הָלַךְ לְשָׁם לְהִשְׁתַּטֵּחַ
עַל קִבְרֵי אָבוֹת – לְהַצִּילוֹ מֵעֲצַת מְרַגְּלִים, וְכֵן מִפֵּרוּשׁ רַשִׁ"י
בְּפָרָשַׁת 'וַיְחִי' עַל פָּסוּק "וַאֲנִי בְּבֹאִי מִפַּדָּן" (בראשית מח,
ז) – וְהוּא גַּם כֵּן מַאֲמַר רַבּוֹתֵינוּ זַ"ל: "וָאֶקְבְּרֶהָ שָׁם" – וְלֹא
הוֹלַכְתִּיהָ אֲפִלּוּ לְבֵית לֶחֶם וְכוּ', וְיָדַעְתִּי שֶׁיֵּשׁ בִּלְבָבְךָ עָלַי, אֲבָל
דַּע לְךָ שֶׁעַל פִּי הַדִּבּוּר קְבַרְתִּיהָ שָׁם – שֶׁתְּהֵא לְעֶזְרָה לְבָנֶיהָ;
כְּשֶׁיִּגְלֶה אוֹתָם נְבוּזַרְאֲדָן, יִהְיוּ עוֹבְרִים דֶּרֶךְ שָׁם, וְיָצְאָה רָחֵל
עַל קְבָרָהּ וּבִכְתָה וּמְבַקֶּשֶׁת עֲלֵיהֶם רַחֲמִים, שֶׁנֶּאֱמַר (ירמיה
לא, יד): 'קוֹל בְּרָמָה נִשְׁמָע' וְגוֹ', וְהַקָּדוֹשׁ בָּרוּךְ הוּא מְשִׁיבָהּ
(שם, טו): יֵשׁ שָׂכָר לִפְעֻלָּתֵךְ נְאֻם ה', וְשָׁבוּ בָנִים לִגְבוּלָם,
עַד כָּאן לְשׁוֹנוֹ:

וּבְמַסֶּכְתָּא סוֹטָה דַּף י"ג אִיתָא: וְאָמַר רַבִּי חָמָא בַּר חֲנִינָא,
מִפְּנֵי מָה נִסְתַּתֵּר קִבְרוֹ שֶׁל מֹשֶׁה מֵעֵינֵי בָשָׂר וָדָם, מִפְּנֵי
שֶׁגָּלוּי וְיָדוּעַ לִפְנֵי הַקָּדוֹשׁ בָּרוּךְ הוּא שֶׁעָתִיד בֵּית הַמִּקְדָּשׁ
לֵחָרֵב וּלְהַגְלוֹת אֶת יִשְׂרָאֵל מֵאַרְצָם, שֶׁמָּא יָבוֹאוּ לִקְבוּרָתוֹ
שֶׁל מֹשֶׁה בְּאוֹתָהּ שָׁעָה וְיַעַמְדוּ בִּבְכִיָּה, וְיִתְחַנְּנוּ לְמֹשֶׁה
וְיֹאמְרוּ לוֹ: מֹשֶׁה רַבֵּנוּ עֲמֹד בִּתְפִלָּה בַּעֲדֵנוּ, וְעוֹמֵד מֹשֶׁה

(Ps. 16:3). All this applies in particular when going to visit their graves, as is implicit in Rashi's commentary (Nu. 13:22) "and he came to Hebron"; "Caleb went there alone to prostrate himself at the graves of the Patriarchs in order to be saved from the counsel of the spies." Similarly, Rashi comments (Gen. 48:7) "and when I came from Padan Aram," "I buried (Rachel) there and I did not take her even as far as Bethlehem, and I know that you reproach me in your heart because of this. But you should know that it was in accordance with God's will that I buried her there in order that she should be of help to her children when Nevuzaradan takes them into exile. They will pass by on the way, and Rachel will come forth from her grave and weep and entreat for mercy on their behalf, as it is written: (Jeremiah, 31, 15ff.) 'A voice is heard in Ramah...' and God answers 'Thy work shall be rewarded, said Hashem' and your children will return to their border.'"

In the Talmud (*Sota* 13a) (see *Ein Ya'acov*), we find: "R. Chama bar Chanina said: "Why was the grave of Moses hidden from the eyes of mankind? Because it was known to the Holy One, blessed-be-He, that the Holy Temple was destined to be destroyed and that Israel would be exiled from their Land. They might have come to the grave of Moses at that moment and stood there weeping and pleading with Moses, saying 'Moses our Teacher, rise and pray for us,' and if Moses had risen to pray, he would have annulled the decree.

וּמְבַטֵּל אֶת הַגְּזֵרָה – מִפְּנֵי שֶׁחֲבִיבִים צַדִּיקִים בְּמִיתָתָם יוֹתֵר מִבְּחַיֵּיהֶם וְכוּ':

מִכָּל זֶה מוּבָן, אֲשֶׁר לִהְיוֹת עַל קִבְרָם מַמָּשׁ, מוֹעִיל בְּיוֹתֵר וְיוֹתֵר מִלְּהַזְכִּיר זְכוּתָם לְבַד וְלִבְלִי לִהְיוֹת עַל קִבְרָם מַמָּשׁ; כִּי גַם לְהַזְכִּיר זְכוּתָם לְבַד גַּם כֵּן גָּדוֹל מְאֹד וּמוֹעִיל מְאֹד, אֲבָל לִהְיוֹת עַל קִבְרָם מַמָּשׁ, זֹאת מוֹעִיל בְּיוֹתֵר וְיוֹתֵר בְּלִי שִׁעוּר, כַּמּוּבָן מִמַּאַמְרֵי חֲכָמֵינוּ ז"ל בִּדְבַר כָּלֵב וְרָחֵל אִמֵּנוּ, וּמִמַּאֲמַר חֲכָמֵינוּ ז"ל מֵהַסְתָּרַת קִבְרוֹ שֶׁל מֹשֶׁה רַבֵּנוּ עָלָיו הַשָּׁלוֹם, וְהָבֵן: כֵּן נִזְכֶּה לֵילֵךְ וּלְהִשְׁתַּטֵּחַ עַל קִבְרֵי הַצַּדִּיקִים, וּלְהַרְבּוֹת בְּעֶתֶר, וְלִשְׁפֹּךְ לִבֵּנוּ כַּמַּיִם נֹכַח פְּנֵי ה', אָז בְּוַדַּאי בָּהֶם עוֹלָם נוֹשַׁע, אָמֵן כֵּן יְהִי רָצוֹן:

Because the Tzadikim are more beloved in their death than in their lifetime."

Rabbi Noson writes: "The Rebbe spoke to me about the Baal Shem Tov's grave, and said it is very good to be there at his graveside. He went on: 'The righteous will inherit the Land' (Psalm 37:29). This means that the true Tzadikim inherit the Land of Israel – their resting place literally has the holiness of the Land of Israel. And the Land of Israel is a great remedy for the abuse of the holy Covenant" (*Likutey Moharan* II 109).

From all this it is clear that to go to their gravesides helps even more than merely invoking their merit alone without visiting their graves. And even merely to mention their name is very great and helps very much. (*Sefer Hamidot*, Tzaddik II 20). May we be worthy of going to prostrate ourselves at the graves of the Tzadikim and offering prayers in abundance and pouring out our hearts before Hashem, and the world will certainly be saved. Amen.

■ ■ ■

**Rebbe Nachman's grave in Uman
(destroyed in World War II)** >

יְהִי רָצוֹן שֶׁאוֹמְרִים קוֹדֶם אֲמִירַת תְּהִלִּים בִּימוֹת הַחוֹל:

יְהִי רָצוֹן מִלְּפָנֶיךָ יְיָ אֱלֹהֵינוּ וֵאלֹהֵי אֲבוֹתֵינוּ, הַבּוֹחֵר בְּדָוִד עַבְדּוֹ וּבְזַרְעוֹ אַחֲרָיו וְהַבּוֹחֵר בְּשִׁירוֹת וְתִשְׁבָּחוֹת, שֶׁתֵּפֶן בְּרַחֲמִים אֶל קְרִיאַת מִזְמוֹרֵי תְהִלִּים שֶׁאֶקְרָא כְּאִלּוּ אֲמָרָם דָּוִד הַמֶּלֶךְ, עָלָיו הַשָּׁלוֹם, בְּעַצְמוֹ זְכוּתוֹ יָגֵן עָלֵינוּ, וְיַעֲמָד לָנוּ זְכוּת פְּסוּקֵי תְהִלִּים וּזְכוּת תֵּבוֹתֵיהֶם וְאוֹתִיּוֹתֵיהֶם וּנְקֻדּוֹתֵיהֶם וְטַעֲמֵיהֶם וְהַשֵּׁמוֹת הַיּוֹצְאִים מֵהֶם מֵרָאשֵׁי תֵבוֹת וּמִסּוֹפֵי תֵבוֹת לְכַפֵּר פְּשָׁעֵינוּ וַעֲוֹנוֹתֵינוּ וְחַטֹּאתֵינוּ וּלְזַמֵּר עָרִיצִים וּלְהַכְרִית כָּל הַחוֹחִים וְהַקּוֹצִים הַסּוֹבְבִים אֶת הַשּׁוֹשַׁנָּה הָעֶלְיוֹנָה וּלְחַבֵּר אֵשֶׁת נְעוּרִים עִם דּוֹדָהּ בְּאַהֲבָה וְאַחֲוָה וְרֵעוּת, וּמִשָּׁם יִמָּשֵׁךְ לָנוּ שֶׁפַע לְנֶפֶשׁ רוּחַ וּנְשָׁמָה לְטַהֲרֵנוּ מֵעֲוֹנוֹתֵינוּ וְלִסְלֹחַ חַטֹּאתֵינוּ וּלְכַפֵּר פְּשָׁעֵינוּ, כְּמוֹ שֶׁסָּלַחְתָּ לְדָוִד שֶׁאָמַר מִזְמוֹרִים אֵלּוּ לְפָנֶיךָ, כְּמוֹ שֶׁנֶּאֱמַר: גַּם יְיָ הֶעֱבִיר חַטָּאתְךָ לֹא תָמוּת. וְאַל תִּקָּחֵנוּ מֵהָעוֹלָם הַזֶּה קֹדֶם זְמַנֵּנוּ עַד מְלֹאת שְׁנוֹתֵינוּ בָּהֶם שִׁבְעִים שָׁנָה בְּאוֹפֶן שֶׁנּוּכַל לְתַקֵּן אֶת אֲשֶׁר שִׁחַתְנוּ . וּזְכוּת דָּוִד הַמֶּלֶךְ, עָלָיו הַשָּׁלוֹם, יָגֵן עָלֵינוּ וּבַעֲדֵנוּ שֶׁתַּאֲרִיךְ אַפְּךָ עַד שׁוּבֵנוּ אֵלֶיךָ בִּתְשׁוּבָה

Prayer before reciting the Psalms:

Our God and God of our fathers:
Who chooses King David and his descendants; Who chooses songs and praises. Please turn to me in mercy and accept the psalms I am going to say as if King David himself were saying them, and let his merit protect us.

There is merit in every verse of the psalms and in every word, in their letters, vowels and notes and in all the holy names spelled out by the first and last letters of each Hebrew word.

Let this merit stand in our favor to atone for our sins and transgressions, cut down our enemies and accusers on High, and destroy all the thorns and thistles surrounding the Supernal Rose. Send down blessing from Your exalted place to all the levels of our soul and spirit, to purify us from our sins, forgive our transgressions and atone for our rebellion, just as You forgave King David who recited these psalms before You. "And Hashem will cause your sin to pass away and you will not die" (Samuel II 12:13).

Do not take us from this world before our time. Give us a full life throughout our span of seventy years so that we can make amends for all the wrong we have done.

May the merit of King David protect us, and be patient with us until we return to You in perfect repentance.

שְׁלֵמָה לְפָנֶיךָ, וּמֵאוֹצַר מַתְּנַת חִנָּם חָנֵּנוּ כְּדִכְתִיב:
וְחַנּוֹתִי אֶת אֲשֶׁר אָחֹן וְרִחַמְתִּי אֶת אֲשֶׁר אֲרַחֵם.
וּכְשֵׁם שֶׁאָנוּ אוֹמְרִים לְפָנֶיךָ שִׁירָה בָּעוֹלָם הַזֶּה כָּךְ
נִזְכֶּה לוֹמַר לְפָנֶיךָ יְיָ אֱלֹהֵינוּ שִׁיר וּשְׁבָחָה לָעוֹלָם הַבָּא,
וְעַל יְדֵי אֲמִירַת תְּהִלִּים תִּתְעוֹרֵר חֲבַצֶּלֶת הַשָּׁרוֹן
וְלָשִׁיר בְּקוֹל נָעִים בְּגִילַת וְרַנֵּן כְּבוֹד הַלְּבָנוֹן נִתַּן לָהּ,
הוֹד וְהָדָר בְּבֵית אֱלֹהֵינוּ, בִּמְהֵרָה בְיָמֵינוּ אָמֵן סֶלָה:

טוב לומר זאת לפני אמירת העשרה מזמורים:

הֲרֵינִי מְקַשֵּׁר עַצְמִי בַּאֲמִירַת הָעֲשָׂרָה מִזְמוֹרִים אֵלּוּ
לְכָל הַצַּדִּיקִים הָאֲמִתִּיִּים שֶׁבְּדוֹרֵנוּ וּלְכָל הַצַּדִּיקִים
הָאֲמִתִּיִּים שׁוֹכְנֵי עָפָר קְדוֹשִׁים אֲשֶׁר בָּאָרֶץ הֵמָּה,
וּבִפְרָט לְרַבֵּנוּ הַקָּדוֹשׁ צַדִּיק יְסוֹד עוֹלָם נַחַל נוֹבֵעַ
מְקוֹר חָכְמָה רַבֵּנוּ נַחְמָן בֶּן פֵיגָא, זְכוּתוֹ יָגֵן עָלֵינוּ,
שֶׁגִּלָּה תִּקּוּן זֶה:

───── HAREINI M'KASHER ─────

he·ma. Oo·bif·rat l'ra·be·nu ha·ka·dosh tza·ddik y'sod o·lam Na·chal
No·ve·ah M'kor Choch·ma, Ra·be·nu Nach·man ben Fei·ga, z'chu·to
ya·gen a·lei·nu v'al Kol Yis·ra·el, A·men:

Grant us blessing from Your treasury of open-handed generosity, as it is written: "I will be gracious to whom I will be gracious, and I will show mercy to whom I will show mercy" (Exodus 33:19). Just as we sing before You in this world, grant us the privilege of singing before You, God, in the World to Come.

Through our recital of the psalms, let pleasant song break forth with rejoicing and exultation. Let glory be given to Israel; and the splendor and beauty shall be in the House of God. Bring it speedily in our days. Amen.

Before reciting the Tikkun HaKlali,
it is good to say the following:

In saying these ten psalms I am binding myself to all the true Tzaddikim in this generation and all the true Tzaddikim who have departed – "the holy ones who are in the earth," and especially to our holy Rebbe, Tzaddik, foundation of the world, the "Flowing Brook, Source of Wisdom," Rebbe Nachman the son of Feige, may his merit protect us, who revealed this remedy.

─────── H A R E I N I   M ' K A S H E R ───────

Ha·rei·ni m'ka·sher atz·mi ba·a·mi·rat a·sa·ra miz·mo·rei T'hi·lim
e·lu l'chol ha-Tza·ddi·kim ha·a·mi·ti·yim she·b'do·re·nu, ool·chol
ha-Tza·ddi·kim ha·a·mi·ti·yim sho·ch'nei a·far k'do·shim a·sher ba·a·retz

קוֹדֶם שֶׁיַּתְחִיל תְּהִלִּים יֹאמַר זֶה:

לְכוּ נְרַנְּנָה לַיְיָ נָרִיעָה לְצוּר יִשְׁעֵנוּ: נְקַדְּמָה פָנָיו בְּתוֹדָה
בִּזְמִירוֹת נָרִיעַ לוֹ: כִּי אֵל גָּדוֹל יְיָ וּמֶלֶךְ גָּדוֹל עַל כָּל
אֱלֹהִים:

הֲרֵינִי מְזַמֵּן אֶת פִּי, לְהוֹדוֹת לְהַלֵּל וּלְשַׁבֵּחַ אֶת
בּוֹרְאִי; לְשֵׁם יִחוּד קֻדְשָׁא בְּרִיךְ הוּא וּשְׁכִנְתֵּיהּ, בִּדְחִילוּ
וּרְחִימוּ, עַל יְדֵי הַהוּא טָמִיר וְנֶעֱלָם בְּשֵׁם כָּל יִשְׂרָאֵל.

———— H A R E I N I   M ' Z A M E N ————

Ha·rei·ni m'za·men et pi, l'ho·dot ool·ha·lel ool·sha·be·ach et
bo·r'ee: L'shem yi·chud Kud·sha B'rich Hu oosh·chin·teh, bid·chi·lu
oor·chi·mu, al y'dei ha·hu ta·mir v'ne·e·lam b'shem kol Yis·ra·el:

Before beginning the psalms, say:

Come let us sing to Hashem, let us shout for joy to the Rock of our salvation. Let us come before His presence with thanksgiving; let us sing to Him joyously in song. For Hashem is a great God and a great King over all gods (Psalms 95:1-3).

I prepare my mouth to give thanks and praise to my Creator, to unify the Holy One, blessed-be-He, and His Shechinah in awe and love, through the Hidden and Concealed One, in the name of all Israel.

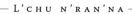

———————— L'CHU N'RAN'NA ————————

L'chu n'ra·n'na l·A·do·nay, na·ri·ah l'tzur yish·e·nu:
N'ka·d'ma fa·nav b'to·dah, biz·mi·rot na·ri·ah lo:
Ki, El ga·dol A·do·nay, oo·me·le·ch ga·dol al kol E·lo·him:

פרק טז

א מִכְתָּם לְדָוִד שָׁמְרֵנִי אֵל, כִּי חָסִיתִי בָךְ:

ב אָמַרְתְּ לַיְיָ אֲדֹנָי אָתָּה, טוֹבָתִי בַּל עָלֶיךָ:

ג לִקְדוֹשִׁים אֲשֶׁר בָּאָרֶץ הֵמָּה, וְאַדִּירֵי כָּל חֶפְצִי בָם:

ד יִרְבּוּ עַצְּבוֹתָם אַחֵר מָהָרוּ, בַּל אַסִּיךְ נִסְכֵּיהֶם מִדָּם, וּבַל אֶשָּׂא אֶת שְׁמוֹתָם עַל שְׂפָתָי:

ה יְיָ מְנָת חֶלְקִי וְכוֹסִי, אַתָּה תּוֹמִיךְ גּוֹרָלִי:

ו חֲבָלִים נָפְלוּ לִי בַּנְּעִימִים, אַף נַחֲלָת שָׁפְרָה עָלָי:

--- PSALM 16 ---

4) Yir·bu atz'vo·tam a·cher ma·ha·ru, bal a·sich nis·kei·hem mi·dam, oo·val esa et sh'mo·tam al s'fa·tay:

5) A·do·nay m'nat chel·ki v'cho·si, a·ta to·mich go·ra·li:

6) Cha·va·lim naf'lu li ban'i·mim, af na·cha·lat sha·f'ra a·lay:

Psalm 16

1   A sweet song of David, a crown for his head. Protect me, God, for I take refuge in You.

2   Community of Israel, say to God: "You are my L-rd, The goodness that You show me is not my due from You, it is because of Your love.

3   Because of the holy ones who rest in the earth and those who were firm in their fear of God – all my desires are fulfilled through their merit.

4   But as for those who hurry after other gods, their afflictions will be multiplied. I will not pour out libations of blood like theirs, I will not bear the names of their gods upon my lips.

5   God, my lot and my portion, cup of my abundance, You have guided me to choose a goodly portion: faith in God.

6   My lot has fallen in places of pleasantness, mine is an inheritance of grace and beauty."

──────────────── P S A L M 1 6 ────────────────

1) Mich·tam l'Da·vid, Sha·m're·ni El ki cha·si·ti vach:

2) Amart lA·do·nay, A·do·nay a·ta, to·va·ti bal a·le·cha:

3) Lik·do·shim a·sher ba·a·retz he·ma, v'a·di·rei kol chef·tzi vam:

ז אֲבָרֵךְ אֶת יְיָ אֲשֶׁר יְעָצָנִי, אַף לֵילוֹת יִסְּרוּנִי כִלְיוֹתָי:

ח שִׁוִּיתִי יְיָ לְנֶגְדִּי תָמִיד, כִּי מִימִינִי בַּל אֶמּוֹט:

ט לָכֵן שָׂמַח לִבִּי וַיָּגֶל כְּבוֹדִי, אַף בְּשָׂרִי יִשְׁכֹּן לָבֶטַח:

י כִּי לֹא תַעֲזֹב נַפְשִׁי לִשְׁאוֹל, לֹא תִתֵּן חֲסִידְךָ לִרְאוֹת שָׁחַת:

יא תּוֹדִיעֵנִי אֹרַח חַיִּים שֹׂבַע שְׂמָחוֹת אֶת פָּנֶיךָ, נְעִימוֹת בִּימִינְךָ נֶצַח:

--------- PSALM 16 ---------

10) Ki lo ta·a·zov naf·shi lish·ol, lo ti·ten cha·si·d'cha lir·ot sha·chat:

11) To·di·e·ni o·rach cha·yim, so·va s'ma·chot et pa·ne·cha, n'ee·mot bi·mi·n'cha ne·tzach:

7 As for me, I will bless God, for He guides me to choose life and follow his ways. Even in the night-time, my reins give me counsel in the fear and love of God.

8 I have placed God before me always, He is always at my right hand: I will not stumble.

9 Therefore my heart is joyous, my soul, glory of my being, exults. My very flesh will dwell secure.

10 For You will not cast my soul into hell, You will not allow your devoted one to see destruction.

11 You will teach me the path of life and grant me the ultimate contentment and joy – The joy of Your countenance, the eternal bliss at Your right hand.

——————————— PSALM 16 ———————————

7) A·va·rech et A·do·nay a·sher y'a·tza·ni, af lei·lot yis'ru·ni chil·yo·tay:

8) Shi·vi·ti A·do·nay l'neg·di Ta·mid, ki mi·mi·ni bal e·mot:

9) La·chen sa·mach li·bi, va·ya·gel k'vo·di, af b'sa·ri yish·kon la·ve·tach:

פרק לב

א לְדָוִד מַשְׂכִּיל, אַשְׁרֵי נְשׂוּי פֶּשַׁע כְּסוּי חֲטָאָה:

ב אַשְׁרֵי אָדָם, לֹא יַחְשֹׁב יְיָ לוֹ עָוֹן, וְאֵין בְּרוּחוֹ רְמִיָּה:

ג כִּי הֶחֱרַשְׁתִּי בָּלוּ עֲצָמָי, בְּשַׁאֲגָתִי כָּל הַיּוֹם:

ד כִּי יוֹמָם וָלַיְלָה תִּכְבַּד עָלַי יָדֶךָ, נֶהְפַּךְ לְשַׁדִּי בְּחַרְבֹנֵי קַיִץ סֶלָה:

ה חַטָּאתִי אוֹדִיעֲךָ, וַעֲוֹנִי לֹא כִסִּיתִי, אָמַרְתִּי אוֹדֶה עֲלֵי פְשָׁעַי לַייָ, וְאַתָּה נָשָׂאתָ עֲוֹן חַטָּאתִי סֶלָה:

―――――――――― PSALM 32 ――――――――――

4) Ki yo·mam va·lai·la tich·bad a·lai ya·de·chah, neh·pach l'sha·di b'char·vo·nei ka·yitz se·la:

5) Cha·ta·ti o·di·a·cha va·a·vo·ni lo chi·si·ti, a·mar·ti o·deh a·lei f'sha·ai lA·do·nay v'a·ta na·sa·ta a·von cha·ta·ti se·la:

Psalm 32

1   A song of David to teach wisdom. Happy is
    he whose sin is forgiven and his transgression
    covered over.

2   Happy is the man whose wrong-doing God
    will not hold against him, because he has truly
    repented and he has no intention of deceiving
    either God or man.

3   As long as I kept silent and did not confess my
    sins before you, I became worn down in my
    very essence, groaning all the day in fear of
    punishment.

4   Because day and night Your hand was heavy
    upon me, my vitality turned as dry as the
    parchedness of summer. Selah.

5   Therefore I will acknowledge my transgression;
    I do not hide my wrongdoing. I said I will
    acknowledge my sins before God: And You have
    forgiven my sin and transgression. Selah.

P S A L M   3 2

1) L'Da·vid Mas·kil, ash·rei ne·suy pe·sha k'sui cha·ta·ah:

2) Ash·rei a·dam lo yach·shov A·do·nay lo a·von, v'ein b'ru·cho
   r'mi·ya:

3) Ki he·che·rash·ti ba·lu a·tza·mai b'sha·a·ga·ti kol ha·yom:

ו   עַל זֹאת יִתְפַּלֵּל כָּל חָסִיד אֵלֶיךָ לְעֵת מְצֹא, רַק לְשֵׁטֶף מַיִם רַבִּים אֵלָיו לֹא יַגִּיעוּ:

ז   אַתָּה סֵתֶר לִי*) מִצַּר תִּצְּרֵנִי, רָנֵּי פַלֵּט תְּסוֹבְבֵנִי סֶלָה:

ח   אַשְׂכִּילְךָ וְאוֹרְךָ בְּדֶרֶךְ זוּ תֵלֵךְ, אִיעֲצָה עָלֶיךָ עֵינִי:

ט   אַל תִּהְיוּ כְּסוּס כְּפֶרֶד אֵין הָבִין, בְּמֶתֶג וָרֶסֶן עֶדְיוֹ לִבְלוֹם, בַּל קְרֹב אֵלֶיךָ:

*) אחר אתה סתר לי, צריך להפסיק מעט (ע"י בלקו"מ ח"א סי' רי"ג).

PSALM 32

8)   As·ki·l'cha v'o·r'cha b'de·rech zu te·lech ee·a·tza a·le·cha ei·ni:

9)   Al tih·yu k'sus, k'fe·red ein ha·vin, b'me·teg va·re·sen ed·yo liv·lom bal k'rov e·le·cha:

6 Let everyone who is devoted to You offer this prayer at the moment You are to be found: That when punishments are sent to scour him at least they should not come upon him like a swelling flood of water.

7 You are my refuge; You guard me from the enemy terror. You surround me with the joys of deliverance. Selah.

8 You have said: I will teach you wisdom and light up the path you should travel. With gestures of my eye will I give you counsel.

9 Do not be like a horse or a stubborn mule which do not understand, which do not distinguish between one who wants to help them and one who wants to harm them. Even when you groom and adorn them, you must curb them with bridle and halter so they will not come close and injure you.

───────────── P S A L M   3 2 ─────────────

6) Al zot yit·pa·lel kol Cha·sid e·le·cha l'et m'tzo, rak l'she·tef ma·yim ra·bim ei·lav lo ya·gi·oo:

7) A·ta se·ter li, (pause*) mi·tzar ti·tz're·ni, ro·nei fa·let t'so·ve·ve·ni se·la:

*see Likutey Moharan I, 213.

י   רַבִּים מַכְאוֹבִים לָרָשָׁע וְהַבּוֹטֵחַ בַּיְיָ חֶסֶד יְסוֹבְבֶנּוּ:

יא   שִׂמְחוּ בַיְיָ וְגִילוּ צַדִּיקִים, וְהַרְנִינוּ כָּל יִשְׁרֵי לֵב:

--- P S A L M 3 2 ---

11)   Sim·chu v'A·do·nay v'gi·lu tza·ddi·kim, v'har·ni·nu kol yish·rei lev:

10 The wicked man, who like them, chaffs at suffering, has many troubles. But one who trusts in
God, knowing that all the suffering God sends
is intended to cleanse and refine him, he will be
surrounded with love.

11 Take joy in God, the source of this love. Exult,
you righteous, and shout for joy all who are
upright in their heart.

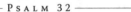

PSALM 32

10)   Ra·bim mach·o·vim la·ra·sha, v'ha·bo·te·ach bA·do·nay che·sed
y'so·v've·nu:

פרק מא

א לַמְנַצֵּחַ מִזְמוֹר לְדָוִד:

ב אַשְׁרֵי מַשְׂכִּיל אֶל דָּל, בְּיוֹם רָעָה יְמַלְּטֵהוּ יְיָ:

ג יְיָ יִשְׁמְרֵהוּ וִיחַיֵּהוּ, וְאֻשַּׁר בָּאָרֶץ, וְאַל תִּתְּנֵהוּ בְּנֶפֶשׁ אֹיְבָיו:

ד יְיָ יִסְעָדֶנּוּ עַל עֶרֶשׂ דְּוָי, כָּל מִשְׁכָּבוֹ הָפַכְתָּ בְחָלְיוֹ:

ה אֲנִי אָמַרְתִּי יְיָ חָנֵּנִי, רְפָאָה נַפְשִׁי כִּי חָטָאתִי לָךְ:

ו אוֹיְבַי יֹאמְרוּ רַע לִי, מָתַי יָמוּת וְאָבַד שְׁמוֹ:

PSALM 41

4) A·do·nay yis·a·de·nu al e·res d'vay kol mish·ka·vo ha·fach·ta b'chol·yo:

5) A·ni a·mar·ti A·do·nay cho·ne·ni, r'fa·ah naf·shi ki cha·ta·ti lach:

6) O·y'vai yo·m'ru ra li, ma·tai ya·mut v'a·vad sh'mo:

Psalm 41

1   For the leader of the singers. A song of David.

2   Happy is he who cares for the poor and sick. On the day of evil God will rescue him.

3   God will guard him and give him life. Throughout the world he will be considered happy. You will not subject him to the desire of his enemies.

4   God will sustain him when he is on his sickbed. Even when he is ill, You attend to him and turn him from one side to the other.

5   But as for me, whom no one comes to visit, I have said: God, have pity. Heal my soul for I have sinned against you.

6   My enemies speak evil against me: "When will he die and his name be destroyed?"

PSALM 41

1) Lam·na·tze·ach miz·mor l'Da·vid:

2) Ash·rei mas·kil el dal, b'yom ra·ah y'ma·l'te·hu A·do·nay:

3) A·do·nay yish·m're·hu vi·cha·ye·hu, v'oo·shar ba·a·retz v'al ti·t'ne·hu b'ne·fesh o·y'vav:

ז וְאִם בָּא לִרְאוֹת, שָׁוְא יְדַבֵּר, לִבּוֹ יִקְבָּץ אָוֶן לוֹ, יֵצֵא לַחוּץ יְדַבֵּר:

ח יַחַד עָלַי יִתְלַחֲשׁוּ כָּל שֹׂנְאָי, עָלַי יַחְשְׁבוּ רָעָה לִי:

ט דְּבַר בְּלִיַּעַל יָצוּק בּוֹ, וַאֲשֶׁר שָׁכַב לֹא יוֹסִיף לָקוּם:

י גַּם אִישׁ שְׁלוֹמִי, אֲשֶׁר בָּטַחְתִּי בוֹ, אוֹכֵל לַחְמִי, הִגְדִּיל עָלַי עָקֵב:

יא וְאַתָּה יְיָ חָנֵּנִי וַהֲקִימֵנִי, וַאֲשַׁלְּמָה לָהֶם:

יב בְּזֹאת יָדַעְתִּי כִּי חָפַצְתָּ בִּי, כִּי לֹא יָרִיעַ אֹיְבִי עָלָי:

PSALM 41
---

10) Gam ish sh'lo·mi a·sher ba·tach·ti bo o·chel lach·mi hig·dil a·lai a·kev:

11) V'a·ta A·do·nay cho·ne·ni v'ha·ki·me·ni, va·a·sha·l'mah la·hem:

12) B'zot ya·da·ti ki cha·fatz·ta bi, ki lo ya·ri·a o·y'vee a·lai:

7 Even if my enemy comes to see, his protestations of concern are false: As he sits there, his heart gathers up malicious thoughts, which he will then go out and spread.

8 All those who hate me whisper together against me and plot evil against me.

9 They say how, "All his evil has now returned on his own head in the form of his illness, and now that he has succumbed, he will never get up again."

10 Even the man I was at peace with, whom I trusted and gave my bread to eat, he has also set up a great ambush about me.

11 But You, O God, take pity on me and raise me up and I shall repay them.

12 By the fact of Your healing me I will know that You have accepted me, if my enemy will not triumph over me.

──────────────── PSALM 41 ────────────────

7) V'eem ba lir·ot shav y'da·ber, li·bo yik·botz a·ven lo, ye·tze la·chutz y'da·ber:

8) Ya·chad a·lai yit·la·cha·shu kol so·n'ay, a·lai yach·sh'vu ra·ah li:

9) D'var b'li·ya·al ya·tzuk bo, va·a·sher sha·chav lo yo·sif la·kum:

יג　וַאֲנִי בְּתֻמִּי, תָּמַכְתָּ בִּי, וַתַּצִּיבֵנִי לְפָנֶיךָ לְעוֹלָם:

יד　בָּרוּךְ יְיָ אֱלֹהֵי יִשְׂרָאֵל מֵהָעוֹלָם וְעַד הָעוֹלָם, אָמֵן וְאָמֵן:

---------- PSALM 41 ----------

14)　Ba·ruch A·do·nay E·lo·hei Yis·ra·el me·ha·o·lam v'ad ha·o·lam
　　　a·men. v'a·men:

13 As for me, it is in my purity that You have supported me and established me before You forever.

14 When I am healed I will praise You: Blessed be Hashem, God of Israel, from eternity to eternity, Amen. Amen.

 ———————— P s a l m 41 ————————

13)   Va·a·ni b'tu·mi ta·mach·ta bi, va·ta·tzi·ve·ni l'fa·ne·chah l'o·lam:

פרק מב

א לַמְנַצֵּחַ מַשְׂכִּיל לִבְנֵי קֹרַח:

ב כְּאַיָּל תַּעֲרֹג עַל אֲפִיקֵי מָיִם, כֵּן נַפְשִׁי תַעֲרֹג אֵלֶיךָ אֱלֹהִים:

ג צָמְאָה נַפְשִׁי לֵאלֹהִים לְאֵל חָי, מָתַי אָבוֹא וְאֵרָאֶה פְּנֵי אֱלֹהִים:

ד הָיְתָה לִּי דִמְעָתִי לֶחֶם יוֹמָם וָלָיְלָה, בֶּאֱמֹר אֵלַי כָּל הַיּוֹם, אַיֵּה אֱלֹהֶיךָ:

ה אֵלֶּה אֶזְכְּרָה וְאֶשְׁפְּכָה עָלַי נַפְשִׁי כִּי אֶעֱבֹר בַּסָּךְ, אֶדַּדֵּם עַד בֵּית אֱלֹהִים בְּקוֹל רִנָּה וְתוֹדָה הָמוֹן חוֹגֵג:

PSALM 42

4) Hay·ta li dim·a·ti le·chem yo·mam va·lai·la, be·e·mor e·lai kol ha·yom a·ye E·lo·he·cha:

5) E·le ez·k'ra v'esh·p'cha a·lai naf·shi ki e·e·vor ba·sach, e·da·dem ad beit E·lo·him b'kol ri·na v'to·da ha'mon cho·geg:

Psalm 42

1 For the leader of the singers. A song of the Sons of Korach. To teach wisdom.

2 As a deer pants for streams of water, so my soul cries out for You, O God.

3 My soul thirsts for God, the living God: when will I come and appear in the presence of God?

4 My tears have been my bread day and night as my enemies taunt me all day long asking: "Where is your God?"

5 This I remember and I pour out my soul within me, how I would go to Jerusalem with the throngs for the Festivals, how I would walk in the procession to the House of God with shouts of joy and thanks to God amidst the Festival crowds.

─────────── P s a l m 4 2 ───────────

1) Lam·na·tze·ach mas·kil liv·nei Ko·rach:

2) K'a·yal ta·a·rog al a·fi·kei ma·yim, ken naf·shi ta·a·rog e·le·cha E·lo·him:

3) Tzam·ah naf·shi lE·lo·him l'El chai, ma·tai a·vo v'e·ra·eh p'nei E·lo·him:

ו מַה תִּשְׁתּוֹחֲחִי נַפְשִׁי וַתֶּהֱמִי עָלָי, הוֹחִלִי
לֵאלֹהִים, כִּי עוֹד אוֹדֶנּוּ יְשׁוּעוֹת פָּנָיו:

ז אֱלֹהַי, עָלַי נַפְשִׁי תִשְׁתּוֹחָח, עַל כֵּן אֶזְכָּרְךָ
מֵאֶרֶץ יַרְדֵּן, וְחֶרְמוֹנִים, מֵהַר מִצְעָר:

ח תְּהוֹם אֶל תְּהוֹם קוֹרֵא לְקוֹל צִנּוֹרֶיךָ, כָּל
מִשְׁבָּרֶיךָ וְגַלֶּיךָ עָלַי עָבָרוּ:

ט יוֹמָם יְצַוֶּה יְיָ חַסְדּוֹ, וּבַלַּיְלָה שִׁירֹה עִמִּי,
תְּפִלָּה לְאֵל חַיָּי:

8) T'hom el t'hom ko·re l'kol tzi·no·re·cha, kol mish·ba·re·cha
v'ga·le·cha a·lai a·va·ru:

9) Yo·mam y'tza·ve A·do·nay chas·do, oo·va·lai·lah shi·ro ee·mi, t'fi·la
l'El cha·yai:

6   Why are you downcast, my soul? Why do you groan within me? Have hope in God. There will come a time when I will give thanks for the salvation which will come from His radiant presence.

7   My God, my soul is downcast in this exile, as I remember Your miracles in the land of Jordan where the River Jordan became dry land at the peaks of Mount Hermon where you passed over our wrong-doing, and at the lowly mountain, Sinai, where you forgave us the sin of the golden calf.

8   Yet in our present exile, deep cries out to deep, one sorrow cries out after another, with the cry from the channels through which You send punishments, which are poured out like water. All Your breakers and waves have swept over me.

9   With the light of day let God command His kindness to be revealed. Even in the night of exile, may His presence rest with me. This is my prayer to the God of my life.

--------------------------- PSALM 42 ---------------------------

6) Mah tish·to·cha·chi naf·shi va·te·he·mi a·lai, ho·chi·li lE·lo·him ki od o·de·nu ye·shu·ot pa·nav:

7) E·lo·hai, a·lai naf·shi tish·to·chach, al ken ez·kor·cha me·e·retz yar·den, v'cher·mo·nim, m'har mitz·ar:

י אוֹמְרָה לְאֵל סַלְעִי לָמָה שְׁכַחְתָּנִי, לָמָה קֹדֵר
אֵלֵךְ, בְּלַחַץ אוֹיֵב:

יא בְּרֶצַח בְּעַצְמוֹתַי חֵרְפוּנִי צוֹרְרָי, בְּאָמְרָם אֵלַי
כָּל הַיּוֹם אַיֵּה אֱלֹהֶיךָ:

יב מַה תִּשְׁתּוֹחֲחִי נַפְשִׁי וּמַה תֶּהֱמִי עָלָי, הוֹחִילִי
לֵאלֹהִים כִּי עוֹד אוֹדֶנּוּ, יְשׁוּעֹת פָּנַי וֵאלֹהָי:

───── PSALM 42 ─────

12) Ma tish'to·cha·chi naf·shi oo·mah te·he·mi a·lai, ho·chi·li lE·lo·him,
ki od o·de·nu, ye·shu·ot pa·nai, vE·lo·hai:

10 I say to God, My Rock, why have You forgotten
    me? Why must I go about in dark gloom under
    the oppression of the enemy?

11 I feel it like murder and the pain of death in my
    bones when my oppressors taunt me and say to
    me all day, "Where is your God?"

12 Why are you downcast, O my soul? Why do
    you groan within me? Have hope in God, for
    I will yet have cause to acknowledge Him, my
    salvation, the light of my face and my God.

PSALM 42

10) O·m'ra l'El sal·ee, la·ma sh'chach·ta·ni la·ma ko·der e·lech
     b'la·chatz o·yev:

11) B're·tzach b'atz·mo·tai, che·r'fu·ni tzo·r'rai, b'o·m'ram e·lai kol
     ha·yom a·ye E·lo·he·chah:

פרק נט

א לַמְנַצֵּחַ אַל תַּשְׁחֵת לְדָוִד מִכְתָּם, בִּשְׁלֹחַ שָׁאוּל וַיִּשְׁמְרוּ אֶת הַבַּיִת לַהֲמִיתוֹ:

ב הַצִּילֵנִי מֵאֹיְבַי אֱלֹהָי, מִמִּתְקוֹמְמַי תְּשַׂגְּבֵנִי:

ג הַצִּילֵנִי מִפֹּעֲלֵי אָוֶן וּמֵאַנְשֵׁי דָמִים הוֹשִׁיעֵנִי:

ד כִּי הִנֵּה אָרְבוּ לְנַפְשִׁי יָגוּרוּ עָלַי עַזִים, לֹא פִשְׁעִי וְלֹא חַטָּאתִי יְיָ:

ה בְּלִי עָוֹן יְרֻצוּן וְיִכּוֹנָנוּ, עוּרָה לִקְרָאתִי וּרְאֵה:

PSALM 59

4) Ki hi·ne a·r'vu l'naf·shi, ya·gu·ru a·lai a·zim, lo fish·ee v'lo cha·ta·ti A·do·nay:

5) B'li a·von y'ru·tzun v'yi·ko·na·nu, oo·rah lik·ra·ti oor·eh:

Psalm 59

1 For the leader of the singers. A precious song of David. "Do not destroy." A prayer composed when Saul sent messengers to wait at the house in order to kill him.

2 Rescue me from my enemies, O my God, give me strength against them that rise up against me.

3 Rescue me from those who act treacherously. Save me from bloodthirsty men.

4 For they are lying in wait for my very soul. Brazen men are gathered against me – and not because of any sin or transgression of mine, O God, You know.

5 Without my having wronged them they come running against me and have readied themselves to kill me. Awaken, come towards me and see.

1) Lam·na·tze·ach al tash·chet l'Da·vid mich·tam, bish·lo·ach Sha·ool va·yish·m'ru et ha·ba·yit la·ha·mito:

2) Ha·tzi·le·ni me·oy'vay E·lo·hai, mi·mit·ko·m'mai t'sa·g've·ni:

3) Ha·tzi·le·ni mi·po·a·lei a·ven, oo·m'an·shei da·mim ho·shi·e·ni:

ו וְאַתָּה יְיָ אֱלֹהִים צְבָאוֹת אֱלֹהֵי יִשְׂרָאֵל,
הָקִיצָה לִפְקֹד כָּל הַגּוֹיִם, אַל תָּחֹן כָּל בֹּגְדֵי
אָוֶן סֶלָה:

ז יָשׁוּבוּ לָעֶרֶב, יֶהֱמוּ כַכָּלֶב, וִיסוֹבְבוּ עִיר:

ח הִנֵּה יַבִּיעוּן בְּפִיהֶם, חֲרָבוֹת בְּשִׂפְתוֹתֵיהֶם, כִּי
מִי שֹׁמֵעַ:

ט וְאַתָּה יְיָ תִּשְׂחַק לָמוֹ, תִּלְעַג לְכָל גּוֹיִם:

י עֻזּוֹ, אֵלֶיךָ אֶשְׁמֹרָה, כִּי אֱלֹהִים מִשְׂגַּבִּי:

יא אֱלֹהֵי חַסְדִּי יְקַדְּמֵנִי, אֱלֹהִים יַרְאֵנִי בְשֹׁרְרָי:

PSALM 59

9) V'a·ta A·do·nay, tis·chak la·mo, til·ag l'chol go·yim:

10) U·zo ei·le·cha esh·mo·rah ki E·lo·him mis·ga·bi:

11) E·lo·hei chas·di y'ka·d'me·ni, E·lo·him yar·e·ni v'sho·r'rai:

6 And You, Lord God of Hosts, the God of Israel, awaken and deal with them just as you deal with all the nations. Show no favor to all who deal treacherously and falsely. Selah.

7 They oppress me in the day, then they are back in the evening. They howl like dogs and go about the city to prevent me escaping.

8 All the day they pour forth slander from their mouths, words sharp as swords are on their lips, for "Who can hear us?" they say.

9 But You, O God, laugh at them, as you scorn all the nations.

10 In the face of the enemy power, I wait for You. For God is my fortress.

11 God, who always shows me love, will send me help in time. He will let me see what I want to happen to those who lie in wait for me.

———————————— P s a l m 5 9 ————————————

6) V'a·ta A·do·nay E·lo·him Tz'va·ot E·lo·hei Yis·ra·el, ha·ki·tza lif·kod kol ha·go·yim, al ta·chon kol bog·dei a·ven se·la:

7) Ya·shu·vu la·e·rev, ye·he·mu cha·ka·lev, vi·so·ve·vu ir:

8) Hi·ne ya·bi·oon b'fi·hem, cha·ra·vot b'sif·to·tei·hem ki mi sho·me·ah:

יב　אַל תַּהַרְגֵם, פֶּן יִשְׁכְּחוּ עַמִּי, הֲנִיעֵמוֹ בְחֵילְךָ
וְהוֹרִידֵמוֹ, מָגִנֵּנוּ אֲדֹנָי:

יג　חַטַּאת פִּימוֹ דְּבַר שְׂפָתֵימוֹ וְיִלָּכְדוּ בִגְאוֹנָם,
וּמֵאָלָה וּמִכַּחַשׁ יְסַפֵּרוּ:

יד　כַּלֵּה בְחֵמָה, כַּלֵּה וְאֵינֵמוֹ, וְיֵדְעוּ כִּי אֱלֹהִים
מֹשֵׁל בְּיַעֲקֹב, לְאַפְסֵי הָאָרֶץ סֶלָה:

טו　וְיָשֻׁבוּ לָעֶרֶב, יֶהֱמוּ כַכָּלֶב, וִיסוֹבְבוּ עִיר:

טז　הֵמָּה יְנִיעוּן לֶאֱכֹל, אִם לֹא יִשְׂבְּעוּ וַיָּלִינוּ:

PSALM 59
---

14) Ka·leh v'che·ma, ka·le v'ei·ne·mo v'ye·d'oo ki E·lo·him mo·shel
b'Ya·a·cov l'af·sei ha·a·retz se·la:

15) V'ya·shu·vu la·e·rev, ye·he·mu cha·ka·lev vi·so·v'vu ir:

16) He·ma y'ni·oon le·e·chol eem lo yis·b'oo va·ya·li·nu:

12 Do not kill them, lest their being dead puts them out of mind, and my people will forget. Put them to flight with Your power and put their fortunes into decline, God our Shield, my Master.

13 The sin of their mouth is the word of their lips. They will be trapped through their pride and men will tell of the curse and the weakness that befell them, and people will learn.

14 Destroy them in Your wrath, destroy them and they will be no more, and all will know that God rules over the people of Jacob, God rules to the ends of the earth. Selah.

15 The wicked return in the evening, they howl like dogs and go round the city.

16 They wander round in search of food. Until they are satiated they will not go to sleep. My enemies are like dogs in their search for my harm.

─────────────── P s a l m 5 9 ───────────────

12) Al ta·har·gem pen yish·k'chu a·mi, ha·ni·e·mo v'che·l'chah v'ho·ri·de·mo ma·gi·ne·nu A·do·nay:

13) Cha·tat pi·mo d'var s'fa·te·mo v'yi·la·ch'du vig·o·nam, oo·me·a·lah oo·mi·ka·chash ye·sa·pe·ru:

יז וַאֲנִי אָשִׁיר עֻזֶּךָ, וַאֲרַנֵּן לַבֹּקֶר חַסְדֶּךָ, כִּי הָיִיתָ מִשְׂגָּב לִי, וּמָנוֹס בְּיוֹם צַר לִי:

יח עֻזִּי אֵלֶיךָ אֲזַמֵּרָה, כִּי אֱלֹהִים מִשְׂגַּבִּי אֱלֹהֵי חַסְדִּי:

PSALM 59
---

18)   Oo·zi e·le·cha a·za·me·ra, ki E·lo·him mis·ga·bi E·lo·hei chas·di:

17 But when You save me I will sing in praise of Your strength, and I will exult in the morning over Your love. For You have been a tower of strength and a refuge for me on my day of trouble.

18 You are my strength, to You I will sing, for God is my tower of strength and a God of love to me.

PSALM 59

17) Va·a·ni a·shir oo·ze·cha, va·a·ra·nen la·bo·ker chas·de·cha, ki ha·yi·ta mis·gav li, oo·ma·nos b'yom tzar li:

פרק עז

א לַמְנַצֵּחַ עַל יְדוּתוּן לְאָסָף מִזְמוֹר:

ב קוֹלִי אֶל אֱלֹהִים וְאֶצְעָקָה, קוֹלִי אֶל אֱלֹהִים
וְהַאֲזִין אֵלָי:

ג בְּיוֹם צָרָתִי אֲדֹנָי דָּרָשְׁתִּי, יָדִי לַיְלָה נִגְּרָה וְלֹא
תָפוּג, מֵאֲנָה הִנָּחֵם נַפְשִׁי:

ד אֶזְכְּרָה אֱלֹהִים וְאֶהֱמָיָה, אָשִׂיחָה, וְתִתְעַטֵּף
רוּחִי סֶלָה:

ה אָחַזְתָּ שְׁמֻרוֹת עֵינָי, נִפְעַמְתִּי וְלֹא אֲדַבֵּר:

ו חִשַּׁבְתִּי יָמִים מִקֶּדֶם, שְׁנוֹת עוֹלָמִים:

───── PSALM 77 ─────

4) Ez·k'ra E·lo·him v'e·he·ma·ya, a·si·cha v'tit·a·tef ru·chi se·la:

5) A·chaz·ta sh'mu·rot ei·nay nif·am·ti v'lo a·da·ber:

6) Chi·shav·ti ya·mim mi·ke·dem, sh'not o·la·mim:

Psalm 77

1 For the leader of the singers. On the sufferings of Israel: A song of Asaph.

2 I lift my voice to God and cry out to Him, I lift my voice to God and He will turn His ears to hear me.

3 On my day of suffering, Master, I have sought for You. In the night of my exile, my hand – the suffering dealt me – is long drawn out, it does not subside. My soul refuses to be comforted.

4 I remember God; I remember the love He showed me in my time of favor, and I sigh. I reflect on those former kindnesses and my soul languishes. Selah.

5 You have gripped the lids of my eyes. I have no rest from my sorrows. I feel smitten and broken and I cannot speak.

6 I have considered the good You did in the days of old, the years of the ages past.

———————————— P S A L M 7 7 ————————————

1) Lam·na·tze·ach al y'du·tun l'Asaf miz·mor:

2) Ko·li el E·lo·him v'etz·a·ka, ko·li el E·lo·him v'ha·a·zin e·lay:

3) B'yom tza·ra·ti A·do·nay da·rash·ti, ya·di lai·la ni·g'ra v'lo ta·fug, me·a·na hi·na·chem naf·shi:

ז אֶזְכְּרָה נְגִינָתִי בַּלָּיְלָה, עִם לְבָבִי אָשִׂיחָה, וַיְחַפֵּשׂ רוּחִי:

ח הַלְעוֹלָמִים יִזְנַח אֲדֹנָי, וְלֹא יֹסִיף לִרְצוֹת עוֹד:

ט הֶאָפֵס לָנֶצַח חַסְדּוֹ, גָּמַר אֹמֶר לְדֹר וָדֹר:

י הֲשָׁכַח חַנּוֹת אֵל, אִם קָפַץ בְּאַף רַחֲמָיו סֶלָה:

יא וָאֹמַר חַלּוֹתִי הִיא, שְׁנוֹת יְמִין עֶלְיוֹן:

יב אֶזְכּוֹר מַעַלְלֵי יָהּ, כִּי אֶזְכְּרָה מִקֶּדֶם פִּלְאֶךָ:

יג וְהָגִיתִי בְכָל פָּעֳלֶךָ, וּבַעֲלִילוֹתֶיךָ אָשִׂיחָה:

PSALM 77

11) Va·o·mar Cha·lo·ti hi, sh'not y'min el·yon:

12) Ez·kor ma·a·l'lei Yah, ki ez·k'ra mi·ke·dem, pil·e·cha:

13) V'ha·gi·ti v'chol pa·o·le·cha oo·va·a·li·lo·te·cha a·si·cha:

7   In this night of exile, I remember my song – the
    song I sang in the Sanctuary. I ponder in my
    heart and my spirit searches out the ways of
    God, and I ask –

8   How can it be that God will cast off forever and
    not show favor once again as He did in the past.

9   Has His mercy disappeared forever? Has He
    made a final decree for all the generations to
    come that He will not return from His anger?

10 Has God forgotten how to show graciousness?
    Has He shut off His love because of His wrath?

11 But I say, it is to inspire us with awe and bring
    us to repent that the right hand of the supreme
    God has changed from bestowing good.

12 I remember the works of God, I remember Your
    wonders to us in former times.

13 I reflect on Your actions and I meditate on Your
    deeds.

———————————— Psalm 77 ————————————

7) Ez·k'ra n'gi·na·ti ba·lai·la eem l'va·vi a·si·chah, vay·cha·pes ru·chi:

8) Hal·o·la·mim yiz·nach A·do·nay v'lo yo·sif lir·tzot od:

9) He·a·fes la·ne·tzach chas·do, ga·mar o·mer l'dor va·dor:

10) Ha·sha·chach cha·not El, eem ka·fatz b'af ra·cha·mav se·la:

יד   אֱלֹהִים בַּקֹּדֶשׁ דַּרְכֶּךָ, מִי אֵל גָּדוֹל כֵּאלֹהִים:

טו   אַתָּה הָאֵל עֹשֵׂה פֶלֶא, הוֹדַעְתָּ בָעַמִּים עֻזֶּךָ:

טז   גָּאַלְתָּ בִּזְרוֹעַ עַמֶּךָ, בְּנֵי יַעֲקֹב וְיוֹסֵף סֶלָה:

יז   רָאוּךָ מַּיִם אֱלֹהִים, רָאוּךָ מַּיִם יָחִילוּ, אַף יִרְגְּזוּ תְהֹמוֹת:

יח   זֹרְמוּ מַיִם עָבוֹת, קוֹל נָתְנוּ שְׁחָקִים, אַף חֲצָצֶיךָ יִתְהַלָּכוּ:

יט   קוֹל רַעַמְךָ בַּגַּלְגַּל, הֵאִירוּ בְרָקִים תֵּבֵל, רָגְזָה וַתִּרְעַשׁ הָאָרֶץ:

PSALM 77

---

18)   Zo·r'mu ma·yim a·vot, kol na·t'nu sh'cha·kim af cha'tza·tze·cha yit·ha·la·chu:

19)   Kol ra·am·cha ba·gal·gal he·ee·ru v'ra·kim te·vel ra·g'zah va·tir·ash ha'a·retz:

14 God, Your way is to sanctify Your name by executing justice among the nations. Which of their gods is as great as God?

15 You are the God that works wonders. You have made known Your strength among the nations.

16 With an outstretched arm You redeemed Your people, the sons of Jacob and Joseph. Selah.

17 The waters of the Red Sea saw You, God, the waters saw You and were afraid. The deeps were thrown into turmoil.

18 The clouds poured forth water, the Heavens emitted a cry, and Your arrows flew about in the camp of the Egyptians to destroy them.

19 The sound of Your thundering was like a whirlwind. Flashes of lightning lit up the world. The earth trembled and quaked.

――――――――――――― P S A L M 7 7 ―――――――――――――

14) E·lo·him ba·ko·desh dar·ke·cha, mi El ga·dol kE·lo·him:

15) A·ta ha·El o·se phe·le, ho·da·ta va·a·mim oo·ze·cha:

16) Ga·al·ta biz·ro·ah a·me·cha, b'nei Ya·a·cov v'Yo·seph se·la:

17) Ra·oo·cha ma·yim E·lo·him, ra·oo·cha ma·yim ya·chi·lu af yir·g'zu t'ho·mot:

כ בַּיָּם דַּרְכֶּךָ וּשְׁבִילְךָ בְּמַיִם רַבִּים, וְעִקְּבוֹתֶיךָ לֹא נֹדָעוּ:

כא נָחִיתָ כַצֹּאן עַמֶּךָ, בְּיַד מֹשֶׁה וְאַהֲרֹן:

— P S A L M 77 —

21) Na·chi·ta ka·tzon a·me·cha, b'yad Mo·she v'A·ha·ron:

20 Your path was in the sea. Your way was in abundant waters, and Your steps were not visible, because the waters rolled back at once to drown the Egyptians.

21 You led Your people as a flock by the hand of Moses and Aaron.

——————————— P S A L M 7 7 ———————————

20) Ba·yam dar·ke·cha, oo·shvi·l'cha b'ma·yim ra·bim, v'ee·k'vo·te·cha lo no·da·oo:

פרק צ

א תְּפִלָּה לְמֹשֶׁה אִישׁ הָאֱלֹהִים, אֲדֹנָי, מָעוֹן אַתָּה הָיִיתָ לָּנוּ בְּדֹר וָדֹר:

ב בְּטֶרֶם הָרִים יֻלָּדוּ, וַתְּחוֹלֵל אֶרֶץ וְתֵבֵל, וּמֵעוֹלָם עַד עוֹלָם, אַתָּה אֵל:

ג תָּשֵׁב אֱנוֹשׁ עַד דַּכָּא, וַתֹּאמֶר שׁוּבוּ בְנֵי אָדָם:

ד כִּי אֶלֶף שָׁנִים בְּעֵינֶיךָ כְּיוֹם אֶתְמוֹל כִּי יַעֲבֹר, וְאַשְׁמוּרָה בַלָּיְלָה:

ה זְרַמְתָּם, שֵׁנָה יִהְיוּ, בַּבֹּקֶר כֶּחָצִיר יַחֲלֹף:

ו בַּבֹּקֶר יָצִיץ וְחָלָף, לָעֶרֶב יְמוֹלֵל וְיָבֵשׁ:

4) Ki e·lef sha·nim b'ei·ne·cha, k'yom et·mol ki ya·a·vor v'ash·mu·ra va·lai·la:

5) Z'ram·tam she·na yih·yu, ba·bo·ker ke·cha·tzir ya·cha·lof:

6) Ba·bo·ker ya·tzitz v'cha·laf la·e·rev y'mo·lel v'ya·vesh:

Psalm 90

1 A prayer of Moses, man of God, Lord, Your have been a refuge for us in every generation.

2 Before the mountains were born and before You formed the earth and the world, from eternity and forever You are God.

3 You bring man down from his confidence and strength to the point where he is ground down and contrite, and You say: "Return to Me, children of man."

4 For a thousand years are in Your eyes like yesterday when it is past and like a watch in the night.

5 The stream of men's lives is a mere sleep. In the morning he sprouts forth like grass.

6 In the morning he flourishes and sprouts forth. But in the evening he is cut down and withers.

———————————— P S A L M 9 0 ————————————

1) T'fi·la l'Mo·she ish ha'E·lo·him, A·do·nay, ma·on a·ta ha·yi·ta la·nu b'dor va·dor:

2) B'te·rem ha·rim yu·la·du va·t'cho·lel e·retz v'te·vel oo·me·o·lam ad o·lam a·ta El:

3) Ta·shev e·nosh ad da·ka, va·to·mer shu·vu b'nei a·dam:

ז　כִּי כָלִינוּ בְאַפֶּךָ, וּבַחֲמָתְךָ נִבְהָלְנוּ:

ח　שַׁתָּה עֲוֹנֹתֵינוּ לְנֶגְדֶּךָ, עֲלֻמֵנוּ, לִמְאוֹר פָּנֶיךָ:

ט　כִּי כָל יָמֵינוּ פָּנוּ בְעֶבְרָתֶךָ, כִּלִּינוּ שָׁנֵינוּ כְמוֹ הֶגֶה:

י　יְמֵי שְׁנוֹתֵינוּ בָהֶם שִׁבְעִים שָׁנָה, וְאִם בִּגְבוּרֹת שְׁמוֹנִים שָׁנָה, וְרָהְבָּם עָמָל וָאָוֶן, כִּי גָז חִישׁ וַנָּעֻפָה:

יא　מִי יוֹדֵעַ עֹז אַפֶּךָ, וּכְיִרְאָתְךָ עֶבְרָתֶךָ:

יב　לִמְנוֹת יָמֵינוּ כֵּן הוֹדַע, וְנָבִיא לְבַב חָכְמָה:

PSALM 90
---

10) Y'mei sh'no·tei·nu ba·hem shiv·im sha·na, v'im big·vu·rot sh'mo·nim sha·na, v'roh·bam a·mal v'a·ven ki gaz chish va·na·oo·fa:

11) Mi yo·de·ah oz a·pe·cha, ooch·yir·a·t'cha ev·ra·te·cha:

12) Lim·not ya·me·nu ken ho·da, v'na·vi l'vav choch·ma:

7 For in Your wrath we are destroyed. We are confounded by Your anger.

8 You place our sins before You and our hidden deeds in the light of Your countenance.

9 For all our days are passed and gone under the glare of Your anger. We have used up our years and they have passed like a fleeting sound.

10 The days of our years are seventy years, if we have exceptional strength perhaps eighty years, and all their pride and grandeur is mere toil and iniquity, it is gone quickly and we fly away.

11 In such a life, who can acquire any understanding of the strength of Your anger in order to feel the awe which You command, – and according to the awe which You command, so is the power of Your wrath against sinners.

12 According to the number of our days, short as they are, teach us while they are with us, and then we will acquire a heart of wisdom.

———————————— PSALM 90 ————————————

7) Ki cha·li·nu v'a·pe·cha, oo·va·cha·ma·t'cha niv·hal·nu:

8) Sha·ta avo·no·tei·nu l'neg·de·cha, a·lu·me·nu lim·or pa·ne·cha:

9) Ki chol ya·mei·nu pa·nu v'ev·ra·te·cha, ki·li·nu sha·nei·nu k'mo he·ge:

יג שׁוּבָה יְיָ עַד מָתָי, וְהִנָּחֵם עַל עֲבָדֶיךָ:

יד שַׂבְּעֵנוּ בַבֹּקֶר חַסְדֶּךָ, וּנְרַנְּנָה וְנִשְׂמְחָה בְּכָל יָמֵינוּ:

טו שַׂמְּחֵנוּ כִּימוֹת עִנִּיתָנוּ, שְׁנוֹת רָאִינוּ רָעָה:

טז יֵרָאֶה אֶל עֲבָדֶיךָ פָעֳלֶךָ, וַהֲדָרְךָ עַל בְּנֵיהֶם:

יז וִיהִי נֹעַם אֲדֹנָי אֱלֹהֵינוּ עָלֵינוּ, וּמַעֲשֵׂה יָדֵינוּ כּוֹנְנָה עָלֵינוּ, וּמַעֲשֵׂה יָדֵינוּ כּוֹנְנֵהוּ:

— P S A L M 90 —

16) Ye·ra·eh el a·va·de·cha pha·o·le·cha, va·ha·da·r'cha al b'nei·hem:

17) Vi·hi no·am A·do·nay E·lo·hei·nu a·lei·nu, oo·ma·a·se ya·dei·nu ko·n'na a·lei·nu, oo·ma·a·se ya·dei·nu ko·n'ne·hu:

13 Return from the heat of Your anger – how long will You be angry? Take pity on Your servants.

14 Satisfy us with Your love on the morning of our redemption, and we will exult and rejoice all our days, even over the troubles we have endured.

15 Give us joy according to the number of days You afflicted us and years we have seen evil.

16 Let Your work be revealed to Your servants and let the splendor of Your glory be revealed to their children.

17 Let the pleasantness of the presence of Hashem our God rest upon us, and establish the work of our hands – the Temple. Establish the work of our hands – our labor – for good and for blessing.

───────────── P SALM 90 ─────────────

13)   Shu·va A·do·nay ad ma·tai, v'hi·na·chem al a·va·de·cha:

14)   Sa·b'e·nu va·bo·ker chas·de·cha, oo·n'ra·n'na v'nis·m'cha b'chol ya·me·nu:

15)   Sa·m'che·nu ki·mot i·ni·ta·nu, sh'not ra·i·nu ra·ah:

פרק קה

א הוֹדוּ לַיְיָ קִרְאוּ בִּשְׁמוֹ הוֹדִיעוּ בָעַמִּים עֲלִילוֹתָיו:

ב שִׁירוּ לוֹ זַמְּרוּ לוֹ שִׂיחוּ בְּכָל נִפְלְאוֹתָיו:

ג הִתְהַלְלוּ בְּשֵׁם קָדְשׁוֹ, יִשְׂמַח לֵב מְבַקְשֵׁי יְיָ:

ד דִּרְשׁוּ יְיָ וְעֻזּוֹ, בַּקְּשׁוּ פָנָיו תָּמִיד:

ה זִכְרוּ נִפְלְאוֹתָיו, אֲשֶׁר עָשָׂה, מֹפְתָיו וּמִשְׁפְּטֵי פִיו:

ו זֶרַע אַבְרָהָם עַבְדּוֹ, בְּנֵי יַעֲקֹב בְּחִירָיו:

PSALM 105

4) Dir·shu A·do·nay v'oo·zo, ba·k'shu pha·nav ta·mid:

5) Zich·ru nif·l'o·tav a·sher a·sa, mo·f'tav oo·mish·p'tei phiv:

6) Ze·ra Av·ra·ham av·do, b'nei Ya·a·kov b'chi·rav:

Psalm 105

1   Give thanks to God, call upon His name. Make known His acts among the nations.

2   Sing to Him, play instruments for Him. Tell of all His miracles.

3   Take pride in His holy name. Take pride that you have such a God. The heart of those who seek for God will rejoice.

4   Search for God and for the revelation of His might. Seek out His face always.

5   Remember the miracles which He wrought, His wonders and the judgments which He executed upon the nations through the utterance of His mouth.

6   Remember this, you who are the seed of Abraham His servant, the children of Jacob, you, His chosen ones.

--------- P s a l m 1 0 5 ---------

1)   Ho·du LA·do·nay kir·oo vish·mo, ho·di·oo va·a·mim a·li·lo·tav:

2)   Shi·ru Lo Zam'ru Lo, si·chu v'chol nif·l'o·tav:

3)   Hit·ha·l'lu b'shem kod·sho, yis·mach lev m'vak·shei A·do·nay:

ז   הוּא יְיָ אֱלֹהֵינוּ, בְּכָל הָאָרֶץ מִשְׁפָּטָיו:

ח   זָכַר לְעוֹלָם בְּרִיתוֹ, דָּבָר צִוָּה, לְאֶלֶף דּוֹר:

ט   אֲשֶׁר כָּרַת אֶת אַבְרָהָם וּשְׁבוּעָתוֹ לְיִשְׂחָק:

י   וַיַּעֲמִידֶהָ לְיַעֲקֹב לְחֹק, לְיִשְׂרָאֵל בְּרִית עוֹלָם:

יא   לֵאמֹר, לְךָ אֶתֵּן אֶת אֶרֶץ כְּנָעַן, חֶבֶל נַחֲלַתְכֶם:

יב   בִּהְיוֹתָם מְתֵי מִסְפָּר, כִּמְעַט וְגָרִים בָּהּ:

יג   וַיִּתְהַלְּכוּ מִגּוֹי אֶל גּוֹי, מִמַּמְלָכָה אֶל עַם אַחֵר:

יד   לֹא הִנִּיחַ אָדָם לְעָשְׁקָם, וַיּוֹכַח עֲלֵיהֶם מְלָכִים:

──────── P S A L M 105 ────────

11) Le·mor, l'cha e·ten et E·retz K'na·an, che·vel na·cha·lat·chem:

12) Bih'yo·tam m'tei mis·par, kim·at, v'ga·rim ba:

13) Va·yit·ha·l'chu mi·goy el goy, mi·mam·la·cha el am a·cher:

14) Lo hi·ni·ach a·dam l'osh·kam, va·yo·chach a·lei·hem m'la·chim:

7   He is Hashem our God – He whose judgments hold sway throughout the earth.

8   God has remembered the eternal covenant of love He made with His children, the word He commanded to endure to the thousandth generation.

9   This covenant He struck with Abraham; it was His oath to Isaac.

10 He established it as a statute for Jacob, an eternal covenant with Israel.

11 Saying, "To you I will give the land of Canaan as the portion of your inheritance."

12 The covenant was made when our ancestors were small in number, they had scarcely dwelled in the land.

13 They wandered from nation to nation, from one kingdom to another people.

14 He did not let any man oppress them, even kings He rebuked for their sake.

───────────── P S A L M   1 0 5 ─────────────

7)   Hu A·do·nay E·lo·hei·nu, b'chol ha·a·retz mish·pa·tav:

8)   Za·char l'o·lam b'ri·to, da·var tzi·va l'e·lef dor:

9)   A·sher ka·rat et-Av·ra·ham, oosh·vu·a·to l'Yis·chak:

10) Va·ya·a·mi·de·ha l'Ya·a·kov l'chok, l'Yis·ra·el b'rit o·lam:

טו אַל תִּגְּעוּ בִמְשִׁיחָי, וְלִנְבִיאַי אַל תָּרֵעוּ:

טז וַיִּקְרָא רָעָב עַל הָאָרֶץ, כָּל מַטֵּה לֶחֶם, שָׁבָר:

יז שָׁלַח לִפְנֵיהֶם אִישׁ, לְעֶבֶד נִמְכַּר יוֹסֵף:

יח עִנּוּ בַכֶּבֶל רַגְלוֹ, בַּרְזֶל בָּאָה נַפְשׁוֹ:

יט עַד עֵת בֹּא דְבָרוֹ, אִמְרַת יְיָ צְרָפָתְהוּ:

כ שָׁלַח מֶלֶךְ וַיַּתִּירֵהוּ, מֹשֵׁל עַמִּים וַיְפַתְּחֵהוּ:

כא שָׂמוֹ אָדוֹן לְבֵיתוֹ, וּמֹשֵׁל בְּכָל קִנְיָנוֹ:

--- PSALM 105 ---

19) Ad et bo d'va·ro, im·rat A·do·nay tz'ra·fat·hu:

20) Sha·lach me·lech va·ya·ti·re·hu, mo·shel a·mim vay·pha·t'che·hu:

21) Sa·mo a·don l'vei·to, oo·mo·shel b'chol kin·ya·no:

15 "Do not touch my anointed ones, and do not harm my prophets."

16 In order to fulfill His word and exile His people to Egypt, He decreed a famine in the land, and the staff on which the people depended – their bread – he broke completely.

17 Before them he sent a man – Joseph, who was sold as a slave.

18 The Egyptians made him suffer by putting his legs in fetters. His very soul was in chains.

19 Until the time that God's decree came to pass that the Children of Israel should go down to Egypt, God's command was that Joseph be refined through the tests he endured in Egypt.

20 Pharaoh the king sent to loosen his fetters, a ruler over nations it was who released him.

21 He appointed him master over his house and gave him power over all his possessions.

PSALM 105

---

15) Al ti·g'oo vim·shi·chay, v'lin·vi·ay al ta·re·oo;

16) Va·yik·ra ra·av al ha·a·retz, kol ma·te le·chem sha·var:

17) Sha·lach lif·nei·hem ish, l'e·ved nim·kar Yo·seph:

18) Ee·nu va·ke·vel rag·lo, bar·zel ba·ah naf·sho:

כב לֶאְסֹר שָׂרָיו בְּנַפְשׁוֹ, וּזְקֵנָיו יְחַכֵּם:

כג וַיָּבֹא יִשְׂרָאֵל מִצְרָיִם, וְיַעֲקֹב גָּר בְּאֶרֶץ חָם:

כד וַיֶּפֶר אֶת עַמּוֹ מְאֹד, וַיַּעֲצִמֵהוּ מִצָּרָיו:

כה הָפַךְ לִבָּם לִשְׂנֹא עַמּוֹ לְהִתְנַכֵּל בַּעֲבָדָיו:

כו שָׁלַח מֹשֶׁה עַבְדּוֹ, אַהֲרֹן אֲשֶׁר בָּחַר בּוֹ:

כז שָׂמוּ בָם דִּבְרֵי אֹתוֹתָיו, וּמֹפְתִים בְּאֶרֶץ חָם:

כח שָׁלַח חֹשֶׁךְ וַיַּחְשִׁךְ, וְלֹא מָרוּ אֶת דְּבָרוֹ:

כט הָפַךְ אֶת מֵימֵיהֶם לְדָם, וַיָּמֶת אֶת דְּגָתָם:

──────── PSALM 105 ────────

26) Sha·lach Mo·she av·do, A·ha·ron a·sher ba·char bo:
27) Sa·mu vam div·rei o·to·tav, oo·mo·f'tim b'E·retz Cham:
28) Sha·lach cho·shech va·ya·cha·shich, v'lo ma·ru et d'va·ro:
29) Ha·fach et mei·mei·hem l'dam, va·ya·met et d'ga·tam:

22 To bind his ministers to Joseph's soul with ties of love, and he taught wisdom to Pharaoh's wise men.

23 Israel came to Egypt: Jacob dwelled in the land of the descendents of Ham.

24 God caused His nation to be abundantly fruitful, and He made them stronger than their oppressors.

25 He turned their hearts to hate His people and to conspire against His servants.

26 He sent His servant Moses, and Aaron, His chosen one.

27 They performed among them the words of God's signs, miracles in the land of Ham.

28 God sent darkness – and it was dark: the signs God sent were faithful in their mission, they did not rebel against His word.

29 He turned their waters to blood and caused their fish to die.

PSALM 105

22) Le·sor sa·rav b'naf·sho, ooz·kei·nav y'cha·kem:

23) Va·ya·vo Yis·ra·el Mitz·ra·yim, v'Ya·a·kov gar b'E·retz Cham:

24) Va·ye·fer et a·mo m'od, va·ya·a·tzi·me·hu mi·tza·rav:

25) Ha·phach li·bam lis·no a·mo, l'hit·na·kel ba·a·va·dav:

ל שָׁרַץ אַרְצָם צְפַרְדְּעִים, בְּחַדְרֵי מַלְכֵיהֶם:

לא אָמַר, וַיָּבֹא עָרֹב, כִּנִּים, בְּכָל גְּבוּלָם:

לב נָתַן גִּשְׁמֵיהֶם בָּרָד, אֵשׁ לֶהָבוֹת בְּאַרְצָם:

לג וַיַּךְ גַּפְנָם וּתְאֵנָתָם, וַיְשַׁבֵּר עֵץ גְּבוּלָם:

לד אָמַר וַיָּבֹא אַרְבֶּה, וְיֶלֶק, וְאֵין מִסְפָּר:

לה וַיֹּאכַל כָּל עֵשֶׂב בְּאַרְצָם, וַיֹּאכַל פְּרִי אַדְמָתָם:

לו וַיַּךְ כָּל בְּכוֹר בְּאַרְצָם, רֵאשִׁית לְכָל אוֹנָם:

לז וַיּוֹצִיאֵם בְּכֶסֶף וְזָהָב וְאֵין בִּשְׁבָטָיו כּוֹשֵׁל:

PSALM 105

34) A·mar va·ya·voh ar·be, v'ye·lek, v'ein mis·par:

35) Va·yo·chal kol e·sev b'ar·tzam, va·yo·chal p'ri ad·ma·tam:

36) Va·yach kol b'chor b'ar·tzam, re·shit l'chol o·nam:

37) Va·yo·tzi·em b'che·seph v'za·hav, v'ein bish·va·tav ko·shel:

30 Their land swarmed with frogs, even in the chambers of their kings.

31 He spoke, and wild animals came. There were lice throughout their borders.

32 He turned their rains into hail, and a flaming fire descended over their land.

33 The hail smote their vines and their fig-trees and broke the trees within their borders.

34 God spoke, and the locust came, different kinds and without number.

35 They ate up all the plants in their country and ate up the fruit of their land.

36 He smote every first-born in their land, the first of all their strength.

37 And He brought out the Children of Israel with silver and gold. In all their tribes no one stumbled through sin.

───────── PSALM 105 ─────────

30) Sha·ratz ar·tzam tz'phar·d'im, b'chad·rei mal·chei·hem:

31) A·mar va·ya·vo a·rov, kinim, b'chol g'vu·lam:

32) Na·tan gish·mei·hem ba·rad, esh le·ha·vot b'ar·tzam:

33) Va·yach gaf·nam oot·eh·na·tam, vay·sha·ber etz g'vu·lam:

לח שָׂמַח מִצְרַיִם בְּצֵאתָם, כִּי נָפַל פַּחְדָּם עֲלֵיהֶם:

לט פָּרַשׂ עָנָן לְמָסָךְ, וְאֵשׁ לְהָאִיר לָיְלָה:

מ שָׁאַל וַיָּבֵא שְׂלָו וְלֶחֶם שָׁמַיִם יַשְׂבִּיעֵם:

מא פָּתַח צוּר, וַיָּזוּבוּ מָיִם, הָלְכוּ בַּצִּיּוֹת נָהָר:

מב כִּי זָכַר אֶת דְּבַר קָדְשׁוֹ, אֶת אַבְרָהָם עַבְדּוֹ:

מג וַיּוֹצִא עַמּוֹ בְשָׂשׂוֹן, בְּרִנָּה אֶת בְּחִירָיו:

מד וַיִּתֵּן לָהֶם אַרְצוֹת גּוֹיִם, וַעֲמַל לְאֻמִּים יִירָשׁוּ:

מה בַּעֲבוּר יִשְׁמְרוּ חֻקָּיו, וְתוֹרֹתָיו יִנְצֹרוּ, הַלְלוּיָהּ:

PSALM 105

42) Ki za·char et d'var kod·sho, et Av·ra·ham av·do:

43) Va·yo·tzi a·mo b'sa·son, b'ri·na et b'chi·rav:

44) Va·yi·ten la·hem ar·tzot go·yim, va·a·mal l'oo·mim yi·ra·shu:

45) Ba·a·vur yish·m'ru chu·kav, v'to·ro·tav yin·tzo·ru, ha·l'lu·Yah:

38 Egypt rejoiced at their going out, because the fear of Israel had fallen upon them.

39 He spread out a cloud for protection, and sent a pillar of fire to light up the night.

40 The people asked and He brought quails; He satisfied them with the bread of Heaven, the Manna.

41 He opened a rock and water flowed forth, in the parched desert it ran like a river.

42 For He remembered His holy word that He had spoken to Abraham His servant.

43 He brought out His people in gladness, His chosen ones in joy.

44 He gave them the lands of the nations and they inherited the fruit of the labor of the peoples.

45 All this in order that they should keep His statutes and guard His teachings. Halleluyah.

———————————— PSALM 105 ————————————

38) Sa·mach Mitz·ra·yim b'tze·tam, ki na·fal pach·dam a·lei·hem:

39) Pa·ras a·nan l'ma·sach, v'esh l'ha·ir lai·la:

40) Sha·al va·ya·veh s'lav, v'le·chem sha·ma·yim yas·bi·em:

41) Pa·tach tzur va·ya·zu·vu ma·yim, ha·l'chu ba·tzi·yot na·har:

פרק קלז

א עַל נַהֲרוֹת בָּבֶל שָׁם יָשַׁבְנוּ, גַּם בָּכִינוּ בְּזָכְרֵנוּ אֶת צִיּוֹן:

ב עַל עֲרָבִים בְּתוֹכָהּ תָּלִינוּ כִּנֹּרוֹתֵינוּ:

ג כִּי שָׁם, שְׁאֵלוּנוּ שׁוֹבֵינוּ דִּבְרֵי שִׁיר, וְתוֹלָלֵינוּ שִׂמְחָה, שִׁירוּ לָנוּ מִשִּׁיר צִיּוֹן:

ד אֵיךְ נָשִׁיר אֶת שִׁיר יְיָ, עַל אַדְמַת נֵכָר:

ה אִם אֶשְׁכָּחֵךְ יְרוּשָׁלָיִם, תִּשְׁכַּח יְמִינִי:

ו תִּדְבַּק לְשׁוֹנִי לְחִכִּי אִם לֹא אֶזְכְּרֵכִי, אִם לֹא אַעֲלֶה אֶת יְרוּשָׁלַיִם עַל רֹאשׁ שִׂמְחָתִי:

PSALM 137

4) Eich na·shir et shir A·do·nay al ad·mat ne·char:

5) Im esh·ka·chech Y'ru·sha·la·yim, tish·kach y'mi·ni:

6) Tid·bak l'sho·ni l'chi·ki im lo ez·k're·chi, im lo a·a·le et Y'ru·sha·la·yim al rosh sim·cha·ti:

Psalm 137

1   By the waters of Babylon, there we sat and wept as we remembered Zion.

2   On willows there in her midst we hung up our harps.

3   For there our captors asked us to sing, those that scorned us asked us to be happy, saying "Sing us some of the songs of Zion."

4   How can we sing the song of God on foreign soil?

5   If I forget you, Jerusalem, let my right hand forget its skills.

6   Let my tongue cleave to the roof of my mouth if I do not remember You, if I do not place Jerusalem above my chief joy.

PSALM 137

1)   Al na·ha·rot Ba·vel, sham ya·shav·nu, gam ba·chi·nu, b'zoch·re·nu et Tzi·yon:

2)   Al a·ra·vim b'to·chah, ta·li·nu ki·no·ro·tei·nu:

3)   Ki sham, sh'eh·lu·nu sho·vei·nu, div·rei shir, v'to·la·lei·nu sim·cha, shi·ru la·nu mi·shir Tzi·yon:

ז זְכֹר יְיָ לִבְנֵי אֱדוֹם אֵת יוֹם יְרוּשָׁלָיִם, הָאוֹמְרִים
עָרוּ עָרוּ עַד הַיְסוֹד בָּהּ:

ח בַּת בָּבֶל הַשְּׁדוּדָה אַשְׁרֵי שֶׁיְשַׁלֶם לָךְ אֵת
גְּמוּלֵךְ שֶׁגָּמַלְתְּ לָנוּ:

ט אַשְׁרֵי, שֶׁיֹּאחֵז וְנִפֵּץ אֶת עֹלָלַיִךְ אֶל הַסָּלַע:

PSALM 137
---

8)   Bat Ba·vel ha·sh'du·da, ash·rei she·y'sha·lem lach et g'mu·lech
she·ga·malt la·nu:

9)   Ash·rei she·yo·chez, v'ni·petz et o·la·la·yich el ha·sa·la:

7   Remember, O God, what the children of Edom
    did on the day of the destruction of Jerusalem,
    saying "Raze it, raze it completely to its
    foundation."

8   Pride of Babylon, you are destined to be de-
    stroyed. Happy is he that will repay you for the
    way you treated us.

9   Happy is the man who will seize your little ones
    and dash them against the rock.

––––––––––––––––– PSALM 137 –––––––––––––––––

7)   Z'chor A·do·nay liv·nei E·dom et yom Y'ru·sha·la·yim, ha·o·m'rim
     a·ru, a·ru, ad hay·sod bah:

פרק קן

א הַלְלוּיָהּ, הַלְלוּ אֵל, בְּקָדְשׁוֹ, הַלְלוּהוּ בִּרְקִיעַ עֻזּוֹ:

ב הַלְלוּהוּ בִגְבוּרֹתָיו, הַלְלוּהוּ כְּרֹב גֻּדְלוֹ:

ג הַלְלוּהוּ בְּתֵקַע שׁוֹפָר הַלְלוּהוּ בְּנֵבֶל וְכִנּוֹר:

ד הַלְלוּהוּ בְתֹף וּמָחוֹל הַלְלוּהוּ בְּמִנִּים וְעֻגָב:

ה הַלְלוּהוּ בְצִלְצְלֵי שָׁמַע, הַלְלוּהוּ בְּצִלְצְלֵי תְרוּעָה:

ו כֹּל הַנְּשָׁמָה, תְּהַלֵּל יָהּ, הַלְלוּיָהּ:

PSALM 150

4) Ha·l'lu·hu b'tof oo·ma·chol, ha·l'lu·hu b'mi·nim v'oo·gav:

5) Ha·l'lu·hu b'tzil·tz'lei sha·ma, ha·l'lu·hu b'tzil·tz'lei t'ru·ah:

6) Kol ha·n'sha·ma, t'ha·lel Yah ha·l'lu·yah:

Psalm 150

1   Praise God. Praise God in His holy Sanctuary. Praise Him in the firmament of His power.

2   Praise Him for His mighty acts; praise Him and tell of His abundant greatness.

3   Praise Him with the blast of the horn. Praise Him with the harp and the lyre.

4   Praise Him on the drums and with dance. Praise Him with stringed instruments and with the flute.

5   Praise Him with the loud-toned cymbals.

6   Let everything that has breath praise God. Halleluyah.

─────────────── PSALM 150 ───────────────

1)   Ha·l'lu·yah ha·l'lu El b'kod·sho, ha·l'lu·hu bir·ki·ah oo·zo:

2)   Ha·l'lu·hu big·vu·ro·tav, ha·l'lu·hu k'rov gud·lo:

3)   Ha·l'lu·hu b'te·ka sho·far, ha·l'lu·hu b'ne·vel v'chi·nor:

אחר שסיים העשרה מזמורים יאמר שלושה פסוקים אלו:

מִי יִתֵּן מִצִּיּוֹן יְשׁוּעַת יִשְׂרָאֵל בְּשׁוּב יְיָ שְׁבוּת עַמּוֹ יָגֵל יַעֲקֹב
יִשְׂמַח יִשְׂרָאֵל: וּתְשׁוּעַת צַדִּיקִים מֵיְיָ מָעוּזָּם בְּעֵת צָרָה:
וַיַּעְזְרֵם יְיָ וַיְפַלְּטֵם, יְפַלְּטֵם מֵרְשָׁעִים, וְיוֹשִׁיעֵם כִּי חָסוּ בוֹ:

Mɪ ʏɪ·ᴛᴇɴ

Vay·a·z'rem A·do·nay vay·fa·l'tem, y'fa·l'tem me·r'sha·im v'yo·shi·em ki
cha·su vo.

transforms every fiber of our being.

This request of the Rebbe was fulfilled with faithful
simplicity by Rabbi Noson, his closest student. He
wrote a volume of prayers known as *Likutey Tefilot.**

The prayers cover every facet of the life of a Jew and
relate to all aspects of Rebbe Nachman's teachings.

Rabbi Noson was fluent in the Bible and the entire
corpus of religious literature. At every turn his prayers
echo the phrases of the psalms and the prophets in all
their poetic richness and spiritual depth. Yet at the same
time Rabbi Noson expressed himself with such sincerity,
honesty and simplicity that the prayers he wrote speak
for anyone whose soul yearns to draw closer to God.

---

* Translated as *The Fiftieth Gate* by the Breslov Research Institute.

After completing the Psalms, the following is said:

If only the salvation of Israel would come out of Zion, when Hashem will turn the captivity of His People! Jacob will rejoice; Israel will exult. The salvation of the righteous is from Hashem, Who will help them and rescue them. He will rescue them from the wicked and save them, for they trusted in Him.

—————————————— Mi yi·ten ——————————————

Mi yi·ten mi·Tzion y'shu·at Yis·ra·el, b'shuv A·do·nay sh'vut a·mo ya·gel
    Ya·a·cov yis·mach Yis·ra·el:
Ut'shu·at Tza·ddi·kim me·A·do·nay ma·oo·zam b'et tza·ra:

The following prayers were written by Rabbi Noson, for Rebbe Nachman's spiritual path is first and foremost one of prayer and meditation. Prayer is man's channel of communication with God. Through it man opens his heart to God and draws God's light into the world in which he lives, thereby illuminating all the details of his life.

The Rebbe wanted us to "turn the Torah into prayers."[1] On the simplest level this means appealing to God to help us achieve the horizons which our study of the Rebbe's lessons opens up for us. In this way the study of Torah becomes more than merely academic. It is a living, involving experience which touches and

—————————————————————————————

1 *Likutey Moharan* II, 25.

אָשִׁירָה לַייָ בְּחַיָּי, אֲזַמְּרָה לֵאלֹהַי בְּעוֹדִי, יֶעֱרַב עָלָיו שִׂיחִי
אָנֹכִי אֶשְׂמַח בַּייָ: הוֹדוּ לַייָ בְּכִנּוֹר, בְּנֵבֶל עָשׂוֹר זַמְּרוּ לוֹ:
אֱלֹהִים, שִׁיר חָדָשׁ אָשִׁירָה לָךְ בְּנֵבֶל עָשׂוֹר אֲזַמְּרָה לָּךְ: עֲלֵי
עָשׂוֹר וַעֲלֵי נָבֶל, עֲלֵי הִגָּיוֹן בְּכִנּוֹר: כִּי שִׂמַּחְתַּנִי יְיָ בְּפָעֳלֶךָ,
בְּמַעֲשֵׂי יָדֶיךָ אֲרַנֵּן.

רִבּוֹנוֹ שֶׁל עוֹלָם, אֲדוֹן כֹּל, בּוֹרֵא כָל הַנְּשָׁמוֹת, רִבּוֹן כָּל
הַמַּעֲשִׂים, הַבּוֹחֵר בְּשִׁירֵי זִמְרָה, עָזְרֵנִי וְחָנֵּנִי בְּרַחֲמֶיךָ הָרַבִּים
וּבַחֲסָדֶיךָ הָעֲצוּמִים, שֶׁאֶזְכֶּה לְעוֹרֵר וּלְהוֹצִיא וּלְגַלּוֹת כָּל
הָעֲשָׂרָה מִינֵי נְגִינָה שֶׁנֶּאֱמַר בָּהֶם סֵפֶר תְּהִלִּים. וּבִזְכוּת אֵלּוּ
הָעֲשָׂרָה קַפִּיטְל תְּהִלִּים שֶׁאָמַרְתִּי לְפָנֶיךָ, שֶׁהֵם כְּנֶגֶד עֲשָׂרָה
מִינֵי נְגִינָה, שֶׁנֶּאֱמַר בָּהֶם סֵפֶר תְּהִלִּים, שֶׁהֵם: אַשְׁרֵי, בְּרָכָה,
מַשְׂכִּיל, שִׁיר, נִצּוּחַ, נִגּוּן, תְּפִלָּה, הוֹדָאָה, מִזְמוֹר, הַלְלוּיָהּ
– בִּזְכוּת הַמִּזְמוֹרִים וּבִזְכוּת הַפְּסוּקִים וּבִזְכוּת תֵּבוֹתֵיהֶם
וְאוֹתִיּוֹתֵיהֶם וּנְקֻדּוֹתֵיהֶם וְטַעֲמֵיהֶם וְהַשֵּׁמוֹת הַיּוֹצְאִים
מֵהֶם מֵרָאשֵׁי תֵבוֹת וּמִסּוֹפֵי תֵבוֹת, וּבִזְכוּת דָּוִד הַמֶּלֶךְ,

After reciting the Tikkun Klali, it is good to say the
following prayer composed by Rabbi Noson:

"I will sing to God with my life; I will play music for
my God as long as I endure. Let the words of my
prayer be sweet for Him. I will rejoice in God."

"Give thanks to God with the music of the harp,
play to Him on the ten-stringed lyre." "God: Let me sing
a new song for You."

"I will play to You on the ten-stringed instrument,
on the ten-stringed harp; sweet music on the lyre. For
You have made me rejoice, O God, with Your deeds. I
will sing for joy over the works of Your hands."

Master of the Universe. Lord over all. Creator
of all the souls. Master of all that exists. God who
chooses music and song: O God, help me! Your love is
overflowing, Your generosity never ceases. Look on me
with favor. Let me be worthy of arousing the ten forms
of song with which the book of Psalms was composed;
let me be worthy of seeing those forms of song revealed.

I plead to you: In the merit of the ten psalms I have
just recited before You, corresponding to the ten forms
of song, *Ashrei, Brachah, Maskil, Shir, Nitzuach, Nigun,*
Tefilah, Hoda'ah, Mizmor, Halleluyah. In the merit of
these psalms, their verses, their words, their letters,
vowels and notes. In the merit of the holy names spelled
out by the letters at the beginnings of their words and
at the ends of their words. In the merit of King David,
peace be upon him, together with all the ten *Tzadikim*

עָלָיו הַשָּׁלוֹם, עִם כָּל הָעֲשָׂרָה צַדִּיקִים, שֶׁיִּסְדוּ סֵפֶר תְּהִלִּים (וּבִזְכוּת הַצַּדִּיק יְסוֹד עוֹלָם, נַחַל נוֹבֵעַ מְקוֹר חָכְמָה, רַבֵּנוּ נַחְמָן בֶּן פֵיגֶא, זְכוּתוֹ יָגֵן עָלֵינוּ, אֲשֶׁר גִּלָּה וְתִקֵּן לוֹמַר אֵלּוּ הָעֲשָׂרָה קַפִּיטְל תְּהִלִּים בִּשְׁבִיל תִּקּוּן הַבְּרִית) וּבִזְכוּת כָּל הַצַּדִּיקִים וְהַחֲסִידִים הָאֲמִתִּיִּים, תְּזַכֵּנִי וּתְחָנֵּנִי, שֶׁאֶזְכֶּה בְּרַחֲמֶיךָ הָרַבִּים לְהוֹצִיא כָּל הַטִּפּוֹת קֶרִי, שֶׁיָּצְאוּ מִמֶּנִּי לְבַטָּלָה, בֵּין בְּשׁוֹגֵג בֵּין בְּמֵזִיד, בֵּין בְּאֹנֶס בֵּין בְּרָצוֹן, (אִם יֵאָמֵר חַס וְשָׁלוֹם בִּשְׁבִיל מִקְרֶה שֶׁנִּזְדַּמֵּן לוֹ בְּאוֹתוֹ הַלַּיְלָה, יֹאמַר בְּאוֹתוֹ זֶה: וּבִפְרָט כָּל הַטִּפּוֹת שֶׁיָּצְאוּ מִמֶּנִּי בְּלַיְלָה זֹאת עַל־יְדֵי מִקְרֶה־לַיְלָה, שֶׁקָּרָה לִי בַּעֲוֹנוֹתַי הָרַבִּים) כֻּלָּם אֶזְכֶּה, בְּרַחֲמֶיךָ הָרַבִּים וּבְחֶמְלָתְךָ הַגְּדוֹלָה וּבְכֹחֲךָ הַגָּדוֹל, לְהוֹצִיאָם מֵהַקְּלִפּוֹת וּמֵהַסִּטְרִין אַחֲרָנִין, מִכָּל הַמְּקוֹמוֹת שֶׁנָּפְלוּ וְנִתְפַּזְּרוּ וְנָפוֹצוּ וְנִדְחוּ לְשָׁם, וְאַל יִדַּח מִמְּךָ נִדָּח. וְתַכְנִיעַ וּתְשַׁבֵּר וְתַהֲרֹג וְתַעֲקֹר וּתְכַלֶּה וּתְבַטֵּל כָּל הַקְּלִפּוֹת וְכָל הָרוּחִין וְשֵׁדִין וְלֵילִין, שֶׁנַּעֲשׂוּ וְנִבְרְאוּ וְנוֹצְרוּ עַל־יְדֵי אֵלּוּ הַטִּפּוֹת, שֶׁיָּצְאוּ מִמֶּנִּי לְבַטָּלָה, וְתָסִיר מֵהֶם חִיּוּתָם, וְתוֹצִיא וְתִגְזֹל מֵהֶם הַחִיּוּת דִּקְדֻשָּׁה, וְכָל הַנִּיצוֹצוֹת הַקְּדוֹשִׁים שֶׁבָּלְעוּ:

who composed the book of Psalms. In the merit of the "Flowing brook, the source of wisdom,"* the "*Tzadik*, foundation of the universe" – Rebbe Nachman, the son of Feige (may his merit protect us!) who revealed these ten psalms which have the power to restore the purity of the covenant, and who instructed that we should say them. And in the merit of all the true *Tzadikim* and all those who are truly pious: I plead to You, whose love is overflowing: let me be worthy of releasing all the drops of seed which have ever come from me in vain – whether unintentionally or deliberately, under compulsion or willingly... (*If one experienced an emission the previous night, he should add*: and let me release all the drops which passed from me this last night as a result of the pollution which came upon me because of my many sins).

Through Your love and pity, and through Your abundant strength and power, let me release these drops from the *kelipot* and the forces of evil, no matter where they may have fallen, no matter how far they may have been scattered or cast out. Let not the outcast be cast out from You. Humble, break, slaughter, uproot, destroy and nullify all the *kelipot* and all the evil forces and spirits which were created, formed and brought into being by those drops which went from me in vain. Take away their life force. Strip them of the holy vitality and the sparks of light which they have swallowed.

---

* Nachal Novea Mekor Chokhmah (Proverbs 18:4) – the first letters of the Hebrew words spell out NaChMaN

רִבּוֹנוֹ שֶׁל עוֹלָם! אֵל חַי וְקַיָּם, חֵי הַחַיִּים, מָלֵא רַחֲמִים, הַדָּן אֶת כָּל הָעוֹלָם לְכַף זְכוּת תָּמִיד, הֶחָפֵץ חֶסֶד וּמַרְבֶּה לְהֵיטִיב. אָבִי אָבִי, גּוֹאֲלִי וּפוֹדִי. יָדַעְתִּי יְיָ יָדַעְתִּי, כִּי אֲנִי בְּעַצְמִי הֶחָיָּב וְהַפּוֹשֵׁעַ אֲפִלּוּ בְּהַמְּקְרוֹת שֶׁנִּזְדַּמְּנוּ לִי בְּשׁוֹגֵג, כִּי לֹא שָׁמַרְתִּי אֶת הַמַּחֲשָׁבָה כְּלָל וְהִרְהַרְתִּי בַּיּוֹם, עַד שֶׁבָּאתִי לִידֵי טֻמְאָה בַּלַּיְלָה, וְעַל־יְדֵי זֶה קִלְקַלְתִּי מַה שֶּׁקִּלְקַלְתִּי, וְגָרַמְתִּי מַה שֶּׁגָּרַמְתִּי, וְשִׁחַתִּתִי מַה שֶּׁשִּׁחַתִּתִי. אוֹי אוֹי אוֹי, אוֹיָה עַל נַפְשִׁי, אוֹי לְנַפְשִׁי, כִּי גָמַלְתִּי לִי רָעָה.

מַה אֹמַר, מָה אֲדַבֵּר, מָה אֶצְטַדָּק. מַה אֹמַר, מָה אֲדַבֵּר, מָה אֶצְטַדָּק. הָאֱלֹהִים מָצָא אֶת עֲוֹנִי. הִנְנִי לְפָנֶיךָ בְּאַשְׁמָה רַבָּה, הִנְנִי לְפָנֶיךָ מָלֵא בּוּשָׁה וּכְלִמָּה, מָלֵא טִנּוּפִים וְלִכְלוּכִים, מָלֵא תּוֹעֵבוֹת רָעוֹת, וְאֵין שׁוּם לָשׁוֹן בָּעוֹלָם שֶׁאוּכַל לְכַנּוֹת בּוֹ עֹצֶם הָרַחֲמָנוּת שֶׁיֵּשׁ עָלַי, כִּי רַע וָמָר, כִּי נָגַע עַד הַנֶּפֶשׁ, מַר לִי מְאֹד, אָבִי שֶׁבַּשָּׁמַיִם; מַר לִי מְאֹד, רִבּוֹן כָּל הָעוֹלָמִים. רְאֵה אֲנַחְתִּי וְאַנְקָתִי, כִּי נַפְשִׁי מָרָה לִי מְאֹד, עַד אֲשֶׁר אֵינִי יוֹדֵעַ אֵיךְ אֲנִי יָכוֹל לִחְיוֹת מֵעֹצֶם מְרִירוּת נַפְשִׁי, אֲשֶׁר עַד גָּבְהֵי שָׁמַיִם יַגִּיעַ, כִּי קַצְתִּי בְחַיַּי, לָמָּה לִי חַיִּים כָּאֵלֶּה, חַיִּים מָרִים וּמְרוּרִים מִמָּוֶת, אֶת קֻבַּעַת כּוֹס הַתַּרְעֵלָה שָׁתִית, מָצִית, נַפְשִׁי.

Master of the Universe. Living and enduring God, Life of all life:

O God, You are filled with love. At all times You judge the world in the scale of merit. Your desire is for love. The power of Your goodness is so great.

My father, my father. Helper and redeemer.

I know, O God, that I myself am the guilty one. I know I am in the wrong. Because even if the pollution took place unwittingly, it came because I have not guarded my thoughts at all. I entertained thoughts and fantasies in the day, and this is why I came to impurity at night. That is why I did the damage that I did, causing what I caused and destroying what I destroyed. Oy! Oy! Oy! My soul. Poor soul of mine, I have inflicted the evil on myself.

What should I say? How can I justify it? What can I say? How can I justify it? God has found out my sin! Here I am before You, laden with guilt, full of shame and embarrassment, full of filth, dirt and vile impurities. There are no words for the unutterable pity of my state. It is evil. Bitter. The wound goes to the very soul. How great is my bitterness, Father in Heaven! How great is my bitterness, Master of all the worlds! See my groaning and sighing. For my soul is very bitter. I do not know how I can live because of the terrible bitterness of my soul, which rises to the heights of the Heavens. I am sick of my life. What point is there in a life like this? O my soul, you have drunk and drained the cup of reeling woe.

רִבּוֹנוֹ שֶׁל עוֹלָם! אַתָּה לְבַד יָדַעְתָּ רֻבֵּי וְעֹצֶם הַפְּגָמִים הַגְּדוֹלִים, הָעֲצוּמִים וְהַנּוֹרָאִים, שֶׁנַּעֲשִׂים עַל־יְדֵי־זֶה בְּכָל הָעוֹלָמוֹת, וְעַתָּה אֵיךְ אוּכַל לְתַקֵּן זֹאת וּבַמֶּה יִזְכֶּה נַעַר כָּמוֹנִי לְתַקֵּן אֶת אֲשֶׁר שִׁחַתִּי, אַךְ אַף־עַל־פִּי־כֵן יָדַעְתִּי, וַאֲנִי מַאֲמִין בֶּאֱמוּנָה שְׁלֵמָה, כִּי אֵין שׁוּם יֵאוּשׁ בָּעוֹלָם כְּלָל. וַעֲדַיִן יֵשׁ לִי תִּקְוָה, וַעֲדַיִן לֹא אָבְדָה תוֹחַלְתִּי מִיְיָ, כִּי חַסְדֵי יְיָ כִּי לֹא תָמְנוּ, כִּי לֹא כָלוּ רַחֲמָיו.

עַל כֵּן בָּאתִי לְפָנֶיךָ, יְיָ אֱלֹהַי וֵאלֹהֵי אֲבוֹתַי, אֱלֹהֵי אַבְרָהָם, אֱלֹהֵי יִצְחָק וֵאלֹהֵי יַעֲקֹב, אֱלֹהֵי כָּל הַצַּדִּיקִים וְהַחֲסִידִים הָאֲמִתִּיִּים וֵאלֹהֵי כָּל יִשְׂרָאֵל, אֱלֹהֵי הָרִאשׁוֹנִים וְהָאַחֲרוֹנִים, שֶׁתְּרַחֵם עָלַי וְתַעֲשֶׂה אֶת אֲשֶׁר בְּחֻקֶּיךָ אֵלֵךְ וְאֶת מִשְׁפָּטֶיךָ אֶשְׁמֹר, וְתָכֹף אֶת יִצְרִי לְהִשְׁתַּעְבֶּד לָךְ, וְתִגְעַר בְּהַיֵּצֶר הָרָע וּתְגָרְשׁוֹ מִמֶּנִּי מֵעַתָּה וְעַד עוֹלָם, וְתִשְׁמְרֵנִי וְתַצִּילֵנִי וּתְפַלְּטֵנִי מֵעַתָּה מִכָּל מִינֵי הִרְהוּרִים רָעִים וּמִמַּחֲשָׁבוֹת רָעוֹת וּמִפְּגַם הָרְאוּת וּמִפְּגַם הַדִּבּוּר, וְתַצִּילֵנוּ מֵעַתָּה מִכָּל מִינֵי פְּגַם הַבְּרִית שֶׁבָּעוֹלָם בְּמַחֲשָׁבָה, דִּבּוּר וּמַעֲשֶׂה, וְתִהְיֶה עִמִּי תָּמִיד וְתִשְׁמְרֵנִי וְתַצִּילֵנִי מִמִּקְרֶה, בֵּין בַּיּוֹם וּבֵין בַּלַּיְלָה, מֵעַתָּה וְעַד עוֹלָם:

אָבִינוּ, מֶלֶךְ אֵל חַי וְקַיָּם, גּוֹאֵל חָזָק. שִׁטַּחְתִּי אֵלֶיךָ כַפָּי. הַצֵּל הַצֵּל, הוֹשִׁיעָה הוֹשִׁיעָה, הַצֵּל לְקוּחִים לַמָּוֶת, הַצֵּל נִרְדָּף וְחַיָּב כָּמוֹנִי, הַצִּילֵנִי מִן הַשְּׁאוֹל תַּחְתִּיּוֹת. תֶּן לִי תִּקְוָה וְלֹא

Master of the Universe, You alone know the true degree of all the harm that has been done in all the worlds because of this. How can I repair it? How can a simple person like myself make amends for what I have ruined?

And yet I know and believe with perfect faith that there is no despair in the whole world, and therefore I still have hope. I have not lost my hope in God, because God's love will never be exhausted, nor will His pity be spent.

O Lord my God and God of my fathers. God of Abraham, God of Isaac, God of Jacob. God of all the true Tzadikim and the truly pious. God of all Israel, God of the first and the last – I have come before You to ask that You take pity on me. Cause me to walk in Your statutes and keep Your laws. Bend my inclination to submit itself to You. Drive the evil inclination from me now and forever. Protect me and free me from any kind of evil thoughts and fantasies. Stop me abusing the faculty of sight and that of speech. Free me from every possible form of neglect of the Holy Covenant, whether in thought, in speech or in action. Be with me always. Guard me and protect me from pollution both by day and by night from now and forever.

Father and King, Living, enduring God, Redeemer. I spread out my hands to You. Free me, Save me, Free those who are in the grip of death. Save one persecuted and guilt-laden like myself. Save me from the pit of hell.

אֹבֵד, חַס וְשָׁלוֹם, כִּי מַה בֶּצַע בְּדָמִי, בְּרִדְתִּי אֶל שַׁחַת, הֲיוֹדְךָ עָפָר, הֲיַגִּיד אֲמִתֶּךָ. דַּלּוּ עֵינַי לַמָּרוֹם, יְיָ עָשְׁקָה לִּי, עָרְבֵנִי, עֲרֹב עַבְדְּךָ לְטוֹב, אַל יַעַשְׁקֻנִי זֵדִים, כִּי אֵין לִי שׁוּם כֹּחַ אֶלָּא בְּפִי, אֵין לִי שׁוּם מָנוֹס וּמִבְטָח, כִּי אִם עָלֶיךָ לְבַד, עַל חֲסָדֶיךָ הָעֲצוּמִים לְבַד, עַל רַחֲמֶיךָ הַגְּדוֹלִים, עַל חֶמְלָתְךָ הָאֲמִתִּית, עַל חֲנִינוֹתֶיךָ הַנִּצְחִיּוֹת וְעַל כֹּחַ וּזְכוּת הַצַּדִּיקִים, שֶׁשָּׁמְרוּ אֶת הַבְּרִית בְּתַכְלִית הַשְּׁלֵמוּת, שֶׁאֵין שְׁלֵמוּת אַחֲרָיו, בָּהֶם תָּמַכְתִּי יְתֵדוֹתַי, בָּהֶם אֶשְׁעַן וְאֶסָּמֵךְ, בִּזְכוּתָם וְכֹחָם אֶבְטַח וַאֲקַוֶּה, כִּי לֹא תַעֲזֹב נַפְשִׁי לִשְׁאוֹל, לֹא תִתֵּן חֲסִידְךָ לִרְאוֹת שָׁחַת.

אֲהָהּ יְיָ, מַלְּטֵנִי! אֲהָהּ יְיָ, פְּדֵנִי! רְאֵה מִסְכֵּן כָּמוֹנִי טוֹרֵף בְּלֵב יַמִּים, תְּהוֹם אֶל תְּהוֹם קוֹרֵא לְקוֹל צִנּוֹרֶיךָ, כָּל מִשְׁבָּרֶיךָ וְגַלֶּיךָ עָלַי עָבָרוּ, צוֹד צָדוּנִי כַּצִפּוֹר, אֹיְבַי חִנָּם. צָמְתוּ בַבּוֹר חַיָּי, וַיַּדּוּ אֶבֶן בִּי. צָפוּ מַיִם עַל רֹאשִׁי, אָמַרְתִּי נִגְזָרְתִּי. קָרָאתִי שִׁמְךָ, יְיָ, מִבּוֹר תַּחְתִּיּוֹת; קָרָאתִי שִׁמְךָ, יְיָ, מִבּוֹר תַּחְתִּיּוֹת:

Give me hope that I will not be lost, God forbid. "What profit is there in my blood, or if I go down to destruction? Will the dust acknowledge you and tell of Your truth?"

My eyes are raised up to the heights. In this oppression, Lord, stand surety for me. Lord, stand surety for Your servant for good. Let not the arrogant oppress me. I have no strength at all except the strength of my mouth – to ask for Your help. I have nowhere to turn for refuge. I have no-one to trust, except You alone.

On who or what can I rely? On what can I depend? Only on the strength of Your unfailing generosity, on Your abundant love and Your everlasting graciousness. And on the strength and merit of the Tzadikim, who guarded the Covenant with ultimate purity, a purity which has no equal. On them I lean for support. In their merit will I trust and place my hope. For You will not abandon my soul to hell. You will not permit Your pious one to see destruction.

O God, release me! See my wretchedness, cast as I am into the heart of the sea, "Deep calls to deep, woe calls to woe, gushing from Your channels. All Your waves and Your breakers have flowed over me." My enemies have trapped me and snared me like a bird – and for nothing. They have consigned me to the pit and ruined my life. They have cast lots for my life. The waters have flowed over my head. I am cut off. From the depths of the pit I call upon Your name, O God, from the depths of the pit I call upon Your name.

רִבּוֹנוֹ שֶׁל עוֹלָם! רִבּוֹנוֹ שֶׁל עוֹלָם! מָלֵא רַחֲמִים, מָלֵא חֶסֶד חִנָּם, מָלֵא חֲנִינוֹת, מָלֵא רַחֲמָנוּת, מָלֵא טוֹב, מָלֵא רָצוֹן. כְּבָר קִבַּלְנוּ עָלֵינוּ לִקְרֹא אֵלֶיךָ תָּמִיד, וְהִנְנִי מְקַיֵּם קַבָּלָתֵנוּ, וְהִנְנִי קוֹרֵא אֵלֶיךָ מִמָּקוֹם שָׁפָל כָּזֶה, מִמְּקוֹמוֹת מְגֻנִים כָּאֵלֶּה. מִמַּעֲמַקִּים קְרָאתִיךָ, יְיָ, מֵעִמְקֵי עֲמַקִּים, מִן הַמֵּצַר קָרָאתִי יָהּ, עֲנָנִי בַמֶּרְחָב יָהּ. וְאִם בַּעֲווֹנוֹתֵינוּ הָרַבִּים יָרַדְנוּ לְמָקוֹם שֶׁיָּרַדְנוּ, וְיָרַדְנוּ עַכְשָׁו בְּעִקְּבוֹת מְשִׁיחָא לִמְקוֹמוֹת נְמוּכִים וּשְׁפָלִים מְאֹד מְאֹד, שֶׁלֹּא יָרְדוּ יִשְׂרָאֵל לְתוֹכָם מֵעוֹלָם, כְּמוֹ שֶׁכָּתוּב: וַתֵּרֶד פְּלָאִים, אֵין מְנַחֵם לָהּ; אַף־עַל־פִּי־כֵן אֵין אָנוּ מְיָאֲשִׁים עַצְמֵנוּ, חַס וְשָׁלוֹם, בְּשׁוּם אֹפֶן בָּעוֹלָם כְּלָל, כִּי כְּבָר הִבְטַחְתָּנוּ לַהֲשִׁיבֵנוּ מִמְּצוּלוֹת יָם, כְּמוֹ שֶׁכָּתוּב: אָמַר אֲדֹנָי מִבָּשָׁן אָשִׁיב, אָשִׁיב מִמְּצֻלוֹת יָם. וּכְתִיב: וְאַף גַּם זֹאת, בִּהְיוֹתָם בְּאֶרֶץ אֹיְבֵיהֶם לֹא מְאַסְתִּים וְלֹא גְעַלְתִּים לְכַלֹּתָם לְהָפֵר בְּרִיתִי אִתָּם, כִּי אֲנִי יְיָ אֱלֹהֵיהֶם:

רִבּוֹנוֹ שֶׁל עוֹלָם! פְּתַח פִּיךָ לְאִלֵּם כָּמוֹנִי, וְתִשְׁלַח לִי דִּבּוּרִים מִמְּעוֹן קָדְשְׁךָ מִן הַשָּׁמַיִם, בְּאֹפֶן שֶׁאוּכַל לְנַצֵּחַ אוֹתְךָ, לִרְצוֹת וּלְפַיֵּס אוֹתְךָ, שֶׁתְּקַבֵּל בְּרַחֲמֶיךָ הָרַבִּים וּבַחֲסָדֶיךָ הָעֲצוּמִים אֶת אֵלּוּ הָעֲשָׂרָה קַפִּיטְל תְּהִלִּים שֶׁאָמַרְתִּי לְפָנֶיךָ, כְּאִלּוּ אֲמָרָם דָּוִד הַמֶּלֶךְ, עָלָיו הַשָּׁלוֹם, בְּעַצְמוֹ, וְאַף־עַל־פִּי שֶׁאֵינִי

Master of the Universe. God overflowing with love and generosity. God filled with graciousness, goodness and favor. We took it upon ourselves to call to You always. Here I am, keeping to my undertaking. I call to You from this low place, from this place of disgrace. I call to You from the very depths, from the lowest of all depths. "In my distress I called on God, Hashem answered me with enlargement." It is true: we have fallen low because of all our sins. As we stand now at the threshold of the coming of Messiah, we have fallen to the lowest, most wretched of places, where Israel never descended before, as it is written: "She fell astoundingly, there is no helper to comfort her." It is true – and yet in spite of this, we do not despair, God forbid, in any way at all. Because long ago You promised to bring us back even from the depths of the sea. As it is written, "God said: I will bring them from Bashan, I will restore them from the depths of the sea." And it is written, "Even when they are in the land of their enemies, I will not reject them, I will not spurn them or destroy them and break my Covenant with them. For I am Hashem their God."

Master of the Universe. Open Your mouth to one dumb as myself, and send down words from Your holy dwelling place in the Heavens. Send me the words that will make it possible for me to conquer You, to find favor in Your eyes and conciliate You, so that in Your abundant love and generosity You will receive these ten psalms which I have recited before You as if King David

יוֹדֵעַ לְכַוֵּן שׁוּם כַּוָּנָה מֵהַכַּוָּנוֹת הָעֲצוּמוֹת וְהַנּוֹרָאוֹת, שֶׁיֵּשׁ בְּאֵלּוּ הָעֲשָׂרָה מִזְמוֹרִים, יְהִי רָצוֹן מִלְּפָנֶיךָ, יְיָ אֱלֹהַי וֵאלֹהֵי אֲבוֹתַי, שֶׁתְּהֵא חֲשׁוּבָה לְפָנֶיךָ הָאֲמִירָה בְּפֶה לְבַד. כְּאִלּוּ הִשַּׂגְתִּי וְכִוַּנְתִּי כָּל הַסּוֹדוֹת וְהַכַּוָּנוֹת שֶׁיֵּשׁ בָּהֶם, וְיִהְיוּ אֲמָרַי לְרָצוֹן לִפְנֵי אֲדוֹן כֹּל.

וְהִנְנִי מַשְׁלִיךְ יְהָבִי עָלֶיךָ, וְהִנְנִי מְקַשֵּׁר עַצְמִי לְכָל הַצַּדִּיקִים הָאֲמִתִּים שֶׁבְּדוֹרֵנוּ וּלְכָל הַצַּדִּיקִים הָאֲמִתִּים, שׁוֹכְנֵי עָפָר, קְדוֹשִׁים אֲשֶׁר בָּאָרֶץ הֵמָּה (וּבִפְרָט לְהַצַּדִּיק יְסוֹד עוֹלָם, נַחַל נוֹבֵעַ מְקוֹר חָכְמָה, רַבֵּנוּ נַחְמָן בֶּן פֵיגֶא, זְכוּתוֹ יָגֵן עָלֵינוּ, אָמֵן), וְעַל דַּעְתָּם וְעַל כַּוָּנָתָם אָמַרְתִּי כָּל אֵלּוּ הָעֲשָׂרָה קַפִּיטְל תְּהִלִּים, וּבִזְכוּתָם וְכֹחָם אֶזְכֶּה לְעוֹרֵר וּלְגַלּוֹת כָּל הָעֲשָׂרָה מִינֵי נְגִינָה, שֶׁנֶּאֱמַר בָּהֶם סֵפֶר תְּהִלִּים, שֶׁהֵם: שִׁיר פָּשׁוּט, כָּפוּל, מְשֻׁלָּשׁ, מְרֻבָּע, שֶׁהֵם כְּלוּלִים בְּשִׁמְךָ הַמְיֻחָד, הַגָּדוֹל וְהַקָּדוֹשׁ.

וּבִזְכוּת וְכֹחַ הַשְּׁנֵי שֵׁמוֹת הַקְּדוֹשִׁים הָאֵלּוּ בְּמִלּוּאָם, שֶׁהֵם "אֵל אֱלֹהִים" (כָּזֶה): אל"ף למ"ד, אל"ף למ"ד ה"י יו"ד מ"ם, שֶׁהֵם עוֹלִים בְּמִסְפָּר תפ"ה [אַרְבַּע מֵאוֹת שְׁמוֹנִים וְחָמֵשׁ], כְּמִסְפָּר תְּהִלִּ"ים, בְּכֹחַ אֵלּוּ הַשֵּׁמוֹת תְּזַכֵּנִי לְהוֹצִיא כָּל הַטִּפּוֹת קֶרִי לְבַטָּלָה מִבֶּטֶן הַקְּלִפָּה שֶׁבְּלָעָם, אֲשֶׁר מִסְפַּר שְׁמָהּ עִם הָאוֹתִיּוֹת עוֹלֶה תפ"ה [אַרְבַּע מֵאוֹת שְׁמוֹנִים

himself had said them. I do not understand the deep and awesome meanings which lie behind the words of these ten psalms. All I could do was to mouth the words. But let my saying the words be accounted before You as if I had understood and intended all the mystical secrets and meanings contained within them. Let my words find Favor before You, Lord of all things.

I cast my burden upon You. I bind myself to all the true *Tzadikim* who dwell in the dust, to all the holy ones who are in the earth. I bind myself to the "*Tzadik, yesod olam Nachal Noveah M'kor Chachmah*" Rebbe Nachman, the son of Feige, (may his merit protect us). As *they* would have said them, as *they* would have meant them I intended these ten psalms. Through their merit and strength let me be worthy of awakening and seeing revealed the ten forms of song with which the book of Psalms was composed – the simple song, the double song, the tripled and the quadrupled. All of them are contained in the unity of Your great and Holy Name.

When the letters of the two holy names *El* and *Elohim* are spelled out in full, they add up to the *gematria* of 485, which corresponds to the *gematria* of the word Tehilim. In the merit of these two names, make me worthy of releasing all the drops of seed which have gone to waste from the belly of the *kelipah* which consumed them. Because the name of the *kelipah* also adds up to 485, since this *kelipah* is the evil counterpart

וְחָמֵשׁ], שֶׁהִיא בַּקְּלִפָּה כְּנֶגֶד קְדֻשַּׁת סֵפֶר תְּהִלִּים, וּבְכֹחַ אֵלּוּ
הָעֲשָׂרָה מִזְמוֹרֵי תְהִלִּים תְּעוֹרֵר הַשְּׁנֵי הַשֵּׁמוֹת הַקְּדוֹשִׁים "אֵל
אֱלֹהִים", וְתַהֲרֹג, וּתְשַׁבֵּר וְתַכְנִיעַ, וְתַעֲקֹר וּתְכַלֶּה וּתְבַטֵּל אֶת
הַקְּלִפָּה הַזֹּאת שֶׁבִּלְעָם, וְתַכְרִיחַ אוֹתָהּ לְהַפְלִיט כָּל הַטִּפּוֹת
הַקְּדוֹשׁוֹת מִבִּטְנָהּ וְקִרְבָּהּ, וְתִמְחֶה שְׁמָהּ וְזִכְרָהּ מִן הָעוֹלָם,
וּתְקַיֵּם מִקְרָא שֶׁכָּתוּב: חַיִל בָּלַע וַיְקִאֶנּוּ, מִבִּטְנוֹ יוֹרִשֶׁנּוּ אֵל,
וְתַהֲרֹג כָּל הַקְּלִפּוֹת, שֶׁנִּבְרְאוּ עַל־יְדֵי אֵלּוּ הַטִּפּוֹת, וְתוֹצִיא
וְתִגְזֹל מֵהֶם הַחִיּוּת דִּקְדֻשָּׁה, וְכָל הַנִּיצוֹצוֹת הַקְּדוֹשׁוֹת שֶׁבָּלְעוּ
עַל־יְדֵי פְּגַם חֵטְא זֶה, כֻּלָּם תּוֹצִיאֵם, וְתַחֲזֹר וּתְקַבְּצֵם
בִּקְדֻשָּׁה שֵׁנִית, וּתְזַכֵּנוּ לְקַבֵּל עָלֵינוּ עֹל מַלְכוּת שָׁמַיִם בְּאַהֲבָה
תָּמִיד, וְנִזְכֶּה לַעֲסֹק כָּל יָמֵינוּ בַּתּוֹרָה וּתְפִלָּה וּמַעֲשִׂים טוֹבִים
בֶּאֱמֶת וּבְלֵב שָׁלֵם, בְּאֹפֶן שֶׁנִּזְכֶּה לִבְרֹא גוּפִים וְכֵלִים קְדוֹשִׁים
לְכָל הַנְּשָׁמוֹת דְּאָזְלִין עַרְטִילָאִין עַל־יְדֵי עֲווֹנוֹתֵינוּ הָרַבִּים
עַל־יְדֵי פְּגַם הַטִּפּוֹת קֶרִי, שֶׁיָּצְאוּ מִמֶּנִּי לְבַטָּלָה.

רִבּוֹנוֹ שֶׁל עוֹלָם, אַמִּיץ כֹּחַ, וְרַב אוֹנִים! עֲשֵׂה מַה שֶּׁתִּתְעַשֶּׂה
בְּרַחֲמֶיךָ הָרַבִּים בְּאֹפֶן שֶׁנִּזְכֶּה לְתַקֵּן פְּגַם הַבְּרִית, פְּגַם טִפֵּי
הַמֹּחַ, בֵּין מַה שֶּׁפָּגַמְנוּ בָּזֶה בְּשׁוֹגֵג, בֵּין בְּמֵזִיד, בֵּין בְּאֹנֶס, בֵּין
בְּרָצוֹן – עַל הַכֹּל תִּמְחַל וְתִסְלַח לִי, אֱלוֹהַּ סְלִיחוֹת, חַנּוּן

of the holy book of Psalms. Through the strength of these ten psalms arouse the power of these two holy names, *El Elohim*, and slaughter, destroy, humble, uproot, abolish and nullify the *kelipah* which consumed the holy drops of seed. Force it to disgorge all of them from its belly and innards. Blot out its name and memory from the world. Fulfill what is written: "It swallowed valour, but had to vomit it forth. From its very belly God took it away."

Slaughter all the *kelipot* which were brought into being through those drops. Strip away from them the holy vitality which they captured. Whatever sparks of holiness were consumed because of this sin, release them, restore them and gather them together in holiness once again. Make us worthy of taking upon ourselves the yoke of the Kingdom of Heaven with love at all times. Let us be worthy all our days to occupy ourselves with Torah, prayer and good deeds, in truth and with all our hearts. Let us create bodies, holy vessels, for all the souls which have gone naked because of our many sins and through the damage caused by the vain emission of the drops of seed.

Master of the Universe, foremost in power, abundant in strength: do whatever You must to make us worthy of undoing the damage to the Covenant and the damage to our intellect, whether it was done unwittingly or intentionally, whether under compulsion or willingly. God of forgiveness, forgive me. You are gracious and ready to forgive. Let us restore completely what was

הַמַּרְבֶּה לִסְלֹחַ, וְנִזְכֶּה לְתַקֵּן כָּל הַפְּגָמִים בִּשְׁלֵמוּת בְּחַיֵּינוּ
בִּזְכוּת הַצַּדִּיקִים הַקְּדוֹשִׁים אֲשֶׁר בָּאָרֶץ הֵמָּה,

(וְאִם יִהְיֶה עַל קִבְרוֹ הַקָּדוֹשׁ יֹאמַר: וּבִזְכוּת הַצַּדִּיק הַזֶּה
הַשּׁוֹכֵן פֹּה, צַדִּיק יְסוֹד עוֹלָם, נַחַל נוֹבֵעַ מְקוֹר חָכְמָה, אֲשֶׁר
אֲנִי מְכַתֵּת רַגְלַי וְטִלְטַלְתִּי עַצְמִי בְּטִלְטוּל הַקָּשֶׁה בִּשְׁבִיל
לָבוֹא הֵנָּה לְהִשְׁתַּטֵּחַ עַל קֶבֶר הַצַּדִּיק הָאֱמֶת הַקָּדוֹשׁ הַזֶּה,
אֲשֶׁר הִבְטִיחָנוּ בְּחַיָּיו הַקְּדוֹשִׁים לַעֲמֹד בְּעֶזְרָתֵנוּ סֶלָה תָּמִיד,
כְּשֶׁנָּבוֹא עַל קִבְרוֹ הַקָּדוֹשׁ וְנִתֶּן פְּרוּטָה לִצְדָקָה וְנֹאמַר אֵלּוּ
הָעֲשָׂרָה קַפִּיטְל תְּהִלִּים, וְהִנֵּה עָשִׂיתִי מַה שֶּׁמֻּטָּל עָלַי, עֲשֵׂה
מַה שֶּׁעָלֶיךָ).

וּמְחַל לִי, וּסְלַח לִי, וְכַפֵּר לִי עַל כָּל הַחֲטָאִים וְהָעֲווֹנוֹת
וְהַפְּשָׁעִים, שֶׁחָטָאתִי וְשֶׁעָוִיתִי וְשֶׁפָּשַׁעְתִּי לְפָנֶיךָ בְּרַמַ"ח
אֵיבָרַי וּשְׁסַ"ה גִּידַי, בְּמַחֲשָׁבָה, דִּבּוּר וּמַעֲשֶׂה, וּבַחֲמִשָּׁה
חוּשִׁים וּבִשְׁאָר כֹּחוֹת הַגּוּף, וּבִפְרָט מַה שֶּׁחָטָאתִי וּפָשַׁעְתִּי
וּפָגַמְתִּי נֶגְדְּךָ בִּפְגַם הַבְּרִית, שֶׁהוּא כְּלָל כָּל הַתּוֹרָה כֻּלָּהּ, וְהָרַע
בְּעֵינֶיךָ עָשִׂיתִי מִנְּעוּרַי עַד הַיּוֹם הַזֶּה. עַל הַכֹּל תִּמְחַל וְתִסְלַח
וּתְכַפֵּר, מָלֵא רַחֲמִים, וּתְמַלֵּא כָּל הַשֵּׁמוֹת שֶׁפָּגַמְתִּי בְּשִׁמְךָ
הַגָּדוֹל. הֶרֶב כַּבְּסֵנִי מֵעֲוֹנִי וּמֵחַטָּאתִי טַהֲרֵנִי, תְּחַטְּאֵנִי בְאֵזוֹב
וְאֶטְהָר, תְּכַבְּסֵנִי, וּמִשֶּׁלֶג אַלְבִּין, תַּשְׁמִיעֵנִי שָׂשׂוֹן וְשִׂמְחָה,

damaged, let us see it restored in our lifetime through the merit of the holy *Tzadikim* who are in the earth...

(*When this prayer is recited at the graveside of Rebbe Nachman himself, say:* ... and through the merit of the *Tzadik* who dwells here, the *Tzadik yesod olam Nachal Noveah M'kor Chachmah*. I have traveled many miles and endured a hard journey in order to come to pray at the grave of the holy *Tzadik* who lies here, who promised us by his very life that he would be ready to help us at all times, if we come to his holy grave and give one penny to charity and recite these ten psalms. I have done my part. Now do Your part).

Forgive me and cleanse me of all the sins and transgressions I have committed against You with my two hundred and forty-eight limbs and my three hundred and sixty-five sinews, whether in thought or speech or action, with my five senses and with all the other faculties of my body, and especially the sins I have committed in abuse of the Holy Covenant, which is the epitome of the whole Torah. I have done what is evil in Your eyes from my youth up to this very day. Grant forgiveness for everything, O God of Love. Restore all the holy names which I have damaged. Do it for the sake of Your great Name. "Wash me of my sin, purify me of my transgression. Cleanse me with hyssop and I shall be pure. Wash me and I will be whiter than snow.

תָּגֵלְנָה עֲצָמוֹת דִּכִּיתָ, הַסְתֵּר פָּנֶיךָ מֵחֲטָאַי, וְכָל עֲוֹנוֹתַי מְחֵה, מְחֵה פְשָׁעַי לְמַעֲנֶךָ, כָּאָמוּר: אָנֹכִי אָנֹכִי, הוּא מֹחֶה פְשָׁעֶיךָ לְמַעֲנִי, וְחַטֹּאתֶיךָ לֹא אֶזְכֹּר.

וְתִמָּלֵא עָלַי בְּרַחֲמִים, וְתִהְיֶה בְּעֶזְרִי תָּמִיד בִּזְכוּת וְכֹחַ הַצַּדִּיקִים הָאֲמִתִּיִּים, וְתִשְׁמְרֵנִי וְתַצִּילֵנִי תָּמִיד, וְתִתֶּן לִי כֹּחַ לְהִתְגַּבֵּר עַל יִצְרִי וְלָכֹף וּלְשַׁבֵּר אֶת תַּאֲוָתִי, וְלֹא אֶפְגֹּם עוֹד מַה שֶּׁפָּגַמְתִּי, וְלֹא אֶעֱשֶׂה עוֹד הָרָע בְּעֵינֶיךָ, וְלֹא אָשׁוּב עוֹד לְכִסְלָה. אִם אָוֶן פָּעַלְתִּי – לֹא אוֹסִיף, כִּי כְּבָר הִבְטַחְתָּנוּ, שֶׁגַּם עַל זֶה מוֹעִיל תְּפִלָּה וּבַקָּשָׁה לְהִנָּצֵל לְהַבָּא, בְּרַחֲמֶיךָ הָאֲמִתִּיִּים, מִן הַיֵּצֶר הָרָע וְכַת דִּילֵהּ, (אִם יִהְיֶה עַל קִבְרוֹ הַקָּדוֹשׁ יֹאמַר זֶה: וּבִפְרָט עַל מְקוֹם צִיּוּן הַקָּדוֹשׁ הַזֶּה עָזְרֵנִי בִּזְכוּת הַצַּדִּיקִים הַגְּנוּזִים פֹּה).

וְרַחֵם עָלַי, וְתֶן לִי כֹּחַ וּגְבוּרָה מֵאִתְּךָ, שֶׁאֶזְכֶּה לְהִתְגַּבֵּר וְלִכְבֹּשׁ אֶת יִצְרִי תָּמִיד, עַד שֶׁאֶזְכֶּה בְּרַחֲמֶיךָ לְגָרְשׁוֹ וּלְסַלְּקוֹ וּלְבַטְּלוֹ מֵעָלַי לְגַמְרֵי מֵעַתָּה וְעַד עוֹלָם, כִּי כְּבָר כָּלוּ בְיָגוֹן חַיָּי, וּשְׁנוֹתַי בַּאֲנָחָה, כָּשַׁל בַּעֲוֹנִי כֹחִי, וַעֲצָמַי עָשֵׁשׁוּ, עַד אֲשֶׁר כָּשַׁל כֹּחַ הַסַּבָּל. רַחֵם עָלַי, אָבִי, אָב הָרַחֲמָן; רַחֵם עָלַי, שׁוֹמֵעַ תְּפִלָּה; חוּס וַחֲמֹל עָלַי, שׁוֹמֵעַ צְעָקָה, שׁוֹמֵעַ אֲנָחָה, שׁוֹמֵעַ אֲנָקָה, רַחֵם רַחֵם, הַצֵּל הַצֵּל, הוֹשִׁיעָה הוֹשִׁיעָה! אַל יִפֹּל דָּמִי אַרְצָה לְפָנֶיךָ, אַל תִּתֵּן לְשַׁחַת נַפְשִׁי, הַצִּילֵנִי מִדָּמִים, אֱלֹהִים,

Let me hear gladness and joy. Let my crushed bones rejoice. Hide Your face from my transgression and blot out all my sins." Blot out my wrongs for Your sake, as it is said: "I, even I am He that blots out your wrongs for My sake. I will not remember your sins."

Show me love and help me at all times through the merit and strength of the true *Tzadikim*. Guard me always and free me. Give me the strength to master my inclination, to subdue and break my desire, and then I will not repeat the damage I have done, I will no longer do what is evil in Your eyes, I will not return to this foolishness. For in love You have given us Your promise that prayer and entreaty can help to free us from the evil inclination and all that is bound up with it. (*At Rebbe Nachman's grave, say*: And as I stand at this holy place, I ask you to help me through the merit of the *Tzadikim* buried here).

Take pity on me and give me the strength to master my inclination always. And in the end, through Your loving help, I will be worthy of casting it out and obliterating it from myself completely My life has been spent in misery, my years in sighing. My strength has been sapped by my sins, my bones are dried. I have not the strength to hold out. Take pity on me, my Father, loving Father. Take pity on me, You who hears prayer. Have mercy upon me and show compassion, You who hears our cries, our groans and our shrieks. Take pity! Take pity! Free me! Free me! Let my blood not fall to the

אֱלֹהֵי תְשׁוּעָתִי. תְּרַנֵּן לְשׁוֹנִי צִדְקָתֶךָ. חוּסָה עָלַי, כְּרֹב רַחֲמֶיךָ, כְּרֹב חֲסָדֶיךָ, יֶהֱמוּ נָא מֵעֶיךָ וַחֲנִינוֹתֶיךָ עַל עֲלוּב נֶפֶשׁ כָּמוֹנִי, עַל נִרְדָּף כָּמוֹנִי, עַל מְלֻכְלָךְ בַּחֲטָאִים כָּמוֹנִי, עַל חֲסַר דֵּעָה, חֲסַר עֵצָה כָּמוֹנִי, כִּי לְךָ לְבַד עֵינֵינוּ תְלוּיוֹת, לְךָ לְבַד רַעְיוֹנַי צוֹפִיּוֹת, דַּלוּ עֵינַי לַמָּרוֹם, עָזְרָה נָּא, הוֹשִׁיעָה נָּא, חוּס וַחֲמֹל נָא עָלַי וְהוֹשִׁיעֵנִי לָשׁוּב אֵלֶיךָ בִּתְשׁוּבָה שְׁלֵמָה, בֶּאֱמֶת וּבְלֵב שָׁלֵם, וְאֶזְכֶּה לִהְיוֹת תָּמִיד כִּרְצוֹנְךָ הַטּוֹב מֵעַתָּה וְעַד עוֹלָם. כְּחַסְדְּךָ חַיֵּינִי, וְאֶשְׁמְרָה עֵדוּת פִּיךָ, לֵב טָהוֹר בְּרָא לִי אֱלֹהִים, וְרוּחַ נָכוֹן חַדֵּשׁ בְּקִרְבִּי:

וּבְכֵן, יְהִי רָצוֹן מִלְּפָנֶיךָ, יְיָ אֱלֹהֵינוּ וֵאלֹהֵי אֲבוֹתֵינוּ, אֲדוֹן הַשִּׂמְחָה וְהַחֶדְוָה, אֲשֶׁר לְפָנֶיךָ אֵין שׁוּם עַצְבוּת כְּלָל לְעוֹלָם, כְּמוֹ שֶׁכָּתוּב: הוֹד וְהָדָר לְפָנָיו, עֹז וְחֶדְוָה בִּמְקוֹמוֹ, שֶׁתַּעַזְרֵנִי בְּרַחֲמֶיךָ הָעֲצוּמִים וּתְזַכֵּנִי לִהְיוֹת בְּשִׂמְחָה תָּמִיד. מְשַׂמֵּחַ נַפְשׁוֹת עֲגוּמִים, שַׂמַּח נַפְשִׁי הָאֻמְלָלָה מְאֹד, הָעֲלוּבָה מְאֹד, הָעֲיֵפָה וְהַצְּמֵאָה וְהָרְעֵבָה אֵלֶיךָ מְאֹד, הָסֵר מִמֶּנִּי יָגוֹן וַאֲנָחָה, שַׂמַּח נֶפֶשׁ עַבְדֶּךָ, כִּי אֵלֶיךָ, יְיָ, נַפְשִׁי אֶשָּׂא. תּוֹדִיעֵנִי אֹרַח חַיִּים. שֹׂבַע שְׂמָחוֹת אֶת פָּנֶיךָ, נְעִימוֹת בִּימִינְךָ נֶצַח. הָשִׁיבָה

ground before You. Do not send my soul to destruction. Save me from this bloodshed, O God, God of my salvation. Let my tongue exult with Your righteousness. Your love is overflowing, Your generosity is unending. Take pity on me, therefore, and let Your compassion be stirred and your graciousness aroused for a pathetic, shame-laden soul such as myself, persecuted as I am, filthy with sin as I am, foolish and directionless as I am. To You alone our eyes are directed, to You alone do we look for our hope. My eyes look up to the heights. Help God, save me! Please have mercy and take pity upon me and save me. Let me return to You with perfect repentance, in truth and with all my heart. Let me be worthy to be as You want me to be – from now on and for all time. Give me life God of love, and I will observe the testimony of Your mouth. "Create in me a pure heart, God, and renew my strength and spirit within me."

Lord our God and God of our fathers, Lord of bliss and joy, before Whom there is no sadness at all, as it is written: "Splendor and majesty are before Him, strength and joy in His place." God steadfast in love, may it be Your will to help me and make me worthy of always being joyous. You who bring joy to those who are sore at heart, bring joy to my crushed spirit, filled as it is with shame, exhaustion, thirst and hunger for You. Remove from me sadness and grief. Rejoice the soul of Your servant. For to You, God, I lift up my soul. "You teach me the path of life, in Your presence lies true contentment and joy,

לִי שְׂשׂוֹן יִשְׁעֶךָ, וְרוּחַ נְדִיבָה תִסְמְכֵנִי. שַׁבְּעֵנִי מִטּוּבֶךָ, וְשַׂמַּח
נַפְשִׁי בִּישׁוּעָתֶךָ, וְטַהֵר לִבִּי לְעָבְדְּךָ בֶּאֱמֶת. עוּרָה כְבוֹדִי, עוּרָה
הַנֵּבֶל וְכִנּוֹר, אָעִירָה שָּׁחַר.

זַכֵּנוּ לְכָל הָעֲשָׂרָה מִינֵי נְגִינָה דִקְדֻשָּׁה, שֶׁהֵם מַכְנִיעִים
וּמְתַקְּנִים פְּגַם הַבְּרִית, כְּאָמוּר: אֲבָרֵךְ אֶת יְיָ אֲשֶׁר יְעָצָנִי,
אַף לֵילוֹת יִסְּרוּנִי כִלְיוֹתָי. לְדָוִד מַשְׂכִּיל, אַשְׁרֵי נְשׂוּי פֶּשַׁע
כְּסוּי חֲטָאָה. בֵּית וָהוֹן נַחֲלַת אָבוֹת, וּמֵיְיָ אִשָּׁה מַשְׂכָּלֶת.
יוֹמָם יְצַוֶּה יְיָ חַסְדּוֹ, וּבַלַּיְלָה שִׁירֹה עִמִּי, תְּפִלָּה לְאֵל חַיָּי.
לַמְנַצֵּחַ עַל תַּשְׁחֵת לְדָוִד מִכְתָּם בִּשְׁלֹחַ שָׁאוּל וַיִּשְׁמְרוּ אֶת
הַבַּיִת לַהֲמִיתוֹ. אֶזְכְּרָה נְגִינָתִי בַּלָּיְלָה. עִם לְבָבִי אָשִׂיחָה
וַיְחַפֵּשׂ רוּחִי, הֲיֵאָכֵל תָּפֵל מִבְּלִי מֶלַח, אִם יֶשׁ טַעַם בְּרִיר
חַלָּמוּת. פֶּן תִּתֵּן לַאֲחֵרִים הוֹדֶךָ וּשְׁנוֹתֶיךָ לְאַכְזָרִי. וְלֹא
אָמַר, אַיֵּה אֱלוֹהַּ עֹשָׂי נֹתֵן זְמִרוֹת בַּלָּיְלָה, שֶׁקֶר הַחֵן
וְהֶבֶל הַיֹּפִי, אִשָּׁה יִרְאַת יְיָ הִיא תִתְהַלָּל. וְנֶאֱמַר: הַלְלוּיָהּ,
הַלְלוּ אֵל בְּקָדְשׁוֹ, הַלְלוּהוּ בִּרְקִיעַ עֻזּוֹ: הַלְלוּהוּ בִגְבוּרוֹתָיו,
הַלְלוּהוּ כְּרֹב גֻּדְלוֹ, הַלְלוּהוּ בְּתֵקַע שׁוֹפָר, הַלְלוּהוּ בְּנֵבֶל
וְכִנּוֹר: הַלְלוּהוּ בְּתֹף וּמָחוֹל הַלְלוּהוּ בְּמִנִּים וְעֻגָב: הַלְלוּהוּ
בְצִלְצְלֵי שָׁמַע, הַלְלוּהוּ בְּצִלְצְלֵי תְרוּעָה: כֹּל הַנְּשָׁמָה תְּהַלֵּל
יָהּ הַלְלוּיָהּ.

in Your right hand are pleasantness and eternal bliss". "Bring me the joy of Your salvation, sustain me with a generous spirit". Satisfy me with Your good, rejoice my soul with Your salvation and purify my heart to serve You in truth. "Awaken, my glory, awaken, harp and lyre. I shall awaken the dawn".

Let me be worthy of all the ten kinds of holy song, which have the power to undo and correct the damage to the Holy Covenant, as it is written: "I will *bless* God, who guides me. Even during the night my reins instruct me". "A wise song of David: *Happy* is the one whose sin is forgiven and his transgression covered over". "House and riches are the inheritance of fathers; but a *prudent* wife is from Hashem". "By day God commands his love to be revealed, and at night his *song* is with me, a prayer to the God of my life". "For the leader of the singers. 'Do no destroy'. A *precious song* of David when Saul sent and they waited at the house to kill him". "I will remember my *song* in the night, I meditate in my heart and my spirit searches". "Can that which has *no savor* be eaten without salt? Is there taste in the juice of mallows?" "Lest you give of your *glory* to others and your years to the cruel." "And he did not say where is my God, my Maker, who gives *songs* in the night." "Favor is false and beauty is vain. A woman that fears God, she shall be *praised*." And it is said: "*Hallelu-Yah*, praise God in His sanctuary, praise Him in the firmament of His power. Praise Him with the blast of the horn. Praise Him with the harp and

רבּוֹנוֹ שֶׁל עוֹלָם! תְּקַע בְּשׁוֹפָר גָּדוֹל לְחֵרוּתֵנוּ, וְשָׂא נֵס לְקַבֵּץ
גָּלֻיּוֹתֵינוּ וְקָרֵב פְּזוּרֵנוּ מִבֵּין הַגּוֹיִם, וּנְפוּצוֹתֵינוּ כַּנֵּס מִיַּרְכְּתֵי
אָרֶץ: וְקַבֵּץ נִדָּחֵנוּ יַחַד מֵאַרְבַּע כַּנְפוֹת הָאָרֶץ לְאַרְצֵנוּ: וְקַיֵּם
בָּנוּ מִקְרָא שֶׁכָּתוּב: וְשָׁב יְיָ אֱלֹהֶיךָ אֶת שְׁבוּתְךָ וְרִחֲמֶךָ, וְשָׁב
וְקִבֶּצְךָ מִכָּל הָעַמִּים, אֲשֶׁר הֱפִיצְךָ יְיָ אֱלֹהֶיךָ שָׁמָּה. אִם
יִהְיֶה נִדַּחֲךָ בִּקְצֵה הַשָּׁמָיִם, מִשָּׁם יְקַבֶּצְךָ יְיָ אֱלֹהֶיךָ וּמִשָּׁם
יִקָּחֶךָ. וֶהֱבִיאֲךָ יְיָ אֱלֹהֶיךָ אֶל הָאָרֶץ, אֲשֶׁר יָרְשׁוּ אֲבֹתֶיךָ,
וִירִשְׁתָּהּ וְהֵיטִבְךָ, וְהִרְבְּךָ מֵאֲבֹתֶיךָ: וְנֶאֱמַר: נְאֻם יְיָ אֱלֹהִים,
מְקַבֵּץ נִדְחֵי יִשְׂרָאֵל, עוֹד אֲקַבֵּץ עָלָיו לְנִקְבָּצָיו. וְנֶאֱמַר: בּוֹנֵה
יְרוּשָׁלַיִם יְיָ, נִדְחֵי יִשְׂרָאֵל יְכַנֵּס.

וּתְמַהֵר וְתָחִישׁ לְגָאֳלֵנוּ, וְתָבִיא לָנוּ אֶת מְשִׁיחַ צִדְקֵנוּ,
וְתִבְנֶה אֶת בֵּית קָדְשֵׁנוּ וְתִפְאַרְתֵּנוּ, וַהֲבִיאֵנוּ לְצִיּוֹן עִירְךָ
בְּרִנָּה, וְלִירוּשָׁלַיִם בֵּית מִקְדָּשְׁךָ בְּשִׂמְחַת עוֹלָם. כְּמוֹ

the lyre. Praise him with the timbrel and dance. Praise Him with stringed instruments and the flute. Praise Him with the clear-toned cymbals. Praise Him with the loud-sounding cymbals. Let everything that has breath praise God, *Hallelu-Yah*."

Master of the Universe, sound the trumpet of our freedom, and lift up the ensign to gather in our exiles. Draw close those of us who are scattered among the nations, and gather up our distant ones from the ends of the earth. Gather our outcasts from the four corners of the earth and bring them to our Land. Fulfill for us the verse that is written: "Hashem your God will turn your captivity and show love to you and return and gather you from all the peoples to whom Hashem your God scattered you. If there be one of your scattered and cast out to the outermost heavens, even from there Hashem your God will gather you in. He will bring you to the Land which your fathers inherited, and he will give it as your inheritance and do good to you and multiply you more than your ancestors." And it is said: "Hashem God, who gathers in the outcasts of Israel, proclaims: I will gather yet more besides those already gathered." And it is said: "God builds Jerusalem and gathers in the outcasts of Israel."

Hasten to release us, bring us our Righteous Mashiach, rebuild the holy and glorious Temple and bring us to Zion, Your city, in gladness, to Jerusalem, to the House of Your sanctuary, in eternal joy, as it is

שֶׁכָּתוּב: וּפְדוּיֵי יְיָ יְשׁוּבוּן, וּבָאוּ צִיּוֹן בְּרִנָּה, וְשִׂמְחַת עוֹלָם
עַל רֹאשָׁם, שָׂשׂוֹן וְשִׂמְחָה יַשִּׂיגוּ, וְנָסוּ יָגוֹן וַאֲנָחָה: וְנֶאֱמַר:
כִּי בְשִׂמְחָה תֵצֵאוּ, וּבְשָׁלוֹם תּוּבָלוּן, הֶהָרִים וְהַגְּבָעוֹת יִפְצְחוּ
לִפְנֵיכֶם רִנָּה, וְכָל עֲצֵי הַשָּׂדֶה יִמְחֲאוּ כָף.

וְנֶאֱמַר: כִּי נִחַם יְיָ צִיּוֹן, נִחַם כָּל חָרְבוֹתֶיהָ, וַיָּשֶׂם מִדְבָּרָהּ
כְּעֵדֶן וְעַרְבָתָהּ כְּגַן יְיָ, שָׂשׂוֹן וְשִׂמְחָה יִמָּצֵא בָהּ, תּוֹדָה וְקוֹל
זִמְרָה. שִׂמְחוּ בַיְיָ וְגִילוּ צַדִּיקִים, וְהַרְנִינוּ כָּל יִשְׁרֵי לֵב: אוֹר
זָרֻעַ לַצַּדִּיק, וּלְיִשְׁרֵי לֵב שִׂמְחָה. שִׂמְחוּ צַדִּיקִים בַּיְיָ, וְהוֹדוּ
לְזֵכֶר קָדְשׁוֹ, אָמֵן נֶצַח סֶלָה וָעֶד:

written: "God's redeemed will return and come to Zion in gladness, eternal joy upon their heads. They will find bliss and joy. Sadness and grief will be put to flight." And it is said: "For in joy will you go out and in peace will you be brought. The hills and mountains will break forth in joy before you and all the trees of the forest will clap their hands."

And it is said: "For God has comforted Zion, he has comforted all her waste places, he has made her deserts like Paradise, and her wilderness like the Garden of God. Bliss and joy will be found in her, gratitude and sounds of song." "Be joyous, O righteous, and exult in God. Rejoice all you upright in heart. Light is sown for the righteous, for the upright in heart, joy. Rejoice, you righteous, in God, and give thanks to His holy Name." Amen. V'Amen.

■ ■ ■

City of Uman – 1922 ❯

זאת התפילה מצאנו באמתחת הכתבים והיא מעוטת הכמות
ורבת האיכות:

רִבּוֹנוֹ שֶׁל עוֹלָם, עִלַּת הָעִלּוֹת וְסִבַּת כָּל הַסִּבּוֹת אַנְתְּ
לְעֵלָּא. לְעֵלָּא מִן כֹּלָא. וְלֵית לְעֵלָּא מִנָּךְ. דְּלֵית מַחֲשָׁבָה
תְּפִיסָא בָּךְ כְּלָל, וְלָךְ דּוּמִיָּה תְהִלָּה. וּמְרוֹמָם עַל כָּל בְּרָכָה
וּתְהִלָּה. אוֹתְךָ אֶדְרֹשׁ, אוֹתְךָ אֲבַקֵּשׁ, שֶׁתִּפְתּוֹר חֲתִירָה דֶּרֶךְ
כְּבוּשָׁה מֵאִתְּךָ, דֶּרֶךְ כָּל הָעוֹלָמוֹת, עַד הַהִשְׁתַּלְשְׁלוּת שֶׁלִּי,
בַּמָּקוֹם שֶׁאֲנִי עוֹמֵד, כְּפִי אֲשֶׁר נִגְלָה לָךְ, יוֹדֵעַ תַּעֲלוּמוֹת.
וּבַדֶּרֶךְ וְנָתִיב הַזֶּה תָּאִיר עָלַי אוֹרְךָ, לְהַחֲזִירֵנִי בִּתְשׁוּבָה
שְׁלֵמָה לְפָנֶיךָ בֶּאֱמֶת כְּפִי רְצוֹנְךָ בֶּאֱמֶת, כְּפִי רָצוֹן מִבְחַר
הַבְּרוּאִים, לִבְלִי לַחֲשֹׁב בְּמַחֲשַׁבְתִּי שׁוּם מַחֲשֶׁבֶת חוּץ וְשׁוּם
מַחֲשָׁבָה וּבִלְבּוּל, שֶׁהוּא נֶגֶד רְצוֹנְךָ, רַק לְדַבֵּק בְּמַחֲשָׁבוֹת
זַכּוֹת צָחוֹת וּקְדוֹשׁוֹת בַּעֲבוֹדָתְךָ בֶּאֱמֶת בְּהַשָּׂגָתְךָ וּבְתוֹרָתֶךָ.
הַט לִבִּי אֶל עֵדְוֹתֶיךָ, וְתֶן לִי לֵב טָהוֹר לְעָבְדְּךָ בֶּאֱמֶת. ›

*This short but powerful prayer was found amongst a collection
of Rabbi Noson's prayers:*

Master of the Universe, cause of all causes. You are supreme. Beyond everything. Higher than You there is nothing. There is no thought that can grasp You in any way. Before You, silence is praise. For You are exalted above all blessing and praise.

You, I will search after. You, I will entreat. Break open a wide path leading from You, down through all the worlds, level by level, all the way to my level, in the place where I am standing, as it is revealed to You, knower of hidden secrets. Through this track, this pathway, send me Your light so as to bring me to return in perfect repentance before You in truth – in accordance with Your true will, in accordance with the way chosen by the true Tzaddikim.

Let me not entertain a single improper thought in my mind, not a single thought or distraction which is contrary to Your will. Let me only attach myself with pure, clear and holy thoughts to Your service in truth: getting to know Your greatness and being close to Your Torah. Incline my heart to Your testimonies and give me a pure heart to serve You in truth. ❯

וּמִמְּצוּלוֹת יָם תּוֹצִיאֵנִי לְאוֹר גָּדוֹל חִישׁ קַל מְהֵרָה. תְּשׁוּעַת יְיָ כְּהֶרֶף עַיִן, "לָאוֹר בְּאוֹר הַחַיִּים" כָּל יְמֵי הֱיוֹתִי עַל פְּנֵי הָאֲדָמָה; וְאֶזְכֶּה לְחַדֵּשׁ נְעוּרַי, הַיָּמִים שֶׁעָבְרוּ בַּחֹשֶׁךְ, לְהַחֲזִירָם אֶל הַקְּדֻשָּׁה, וְתִהְיֶה יְצִיאָתִי מִן הָעוֹלָם כְּבִיאָתִי, בְּלֹא חֵטְא. וְאֶזְכֶּה לַחֲזוֹת בְּנֹעַם יְיָ וּלְבַקֵּר בְּהֵיכָלוֹ, כֻּלּוֹ אוֹמֵר כָּבוֹד. אָמֵן נֶצַח סֶלָה וָעֶד:

∎ ∎ ∎

Draw me from the depths of the sea to a great light – speedily and quickly. God's salvation can come like the flicker of an eye to let me be illumined with the light of life all the days of my being on the face of the earth. Then I will be worthy of renewing my youth – all the days that passed in darkness. I will be worthy of returning them to holiness. Let my departure from the world be like my coming into it: without sin.

Let me be worthy of gazing on the pleasantness of Hashem and visiting His hall where everything declares "Glory!" Amen. Selah.

Rabbi Tzvi Aryeh Rosenfeld – a pioneer of the Breslov movement in America – and some students on a pilgrimage to Rebbe Nachman's gravesite – 1978

(Courtesy of Reb Aharon Kliger – Breslov Har Hamor)